W9-BBM-489

NOSTALGIA FOR PARADISE

NOSTALGIA
FOR
PARADISE

❖—❖—❖—❖—❖—❖—❖—❖—❖—❖—❖—❖

Sister Sylvia Mary, C. S. M. V.

74524

BR
127
.S9

ST. JOSEPH'S UNIVERSITY

BTQ 22 .S98   STX

Nostalgia for paradise.

3 9353 00006 3956

❖—❖—❖—❖—❖—❖—❖—❖—❖—❖—❖—❖

DESCLEE COMPANY
New York Tournai Paris Rome

NIHIL OBSTAT
J. Roussel, can., libr. cens.
IMPRIMATUR
J. Thomas, vic. gen.
Tornaci, die 17 iulii 1964

© *1965 Sylvia Mary*
Library of Congress Catalogue number 65-15995

Printed and bound in Belgium by Desclee & Cie, Editeurs, Tournai.

CONTENTS

FOR
SAMUEL HENRY HOOKE, D.D.

'It is of Christ alone that Scripture speaks, both in the Old Testament and in the New. He is " the image of the invisible God " (Col. 1: 15) It is from Him that the images and symbols of the Old Testament receive their mysterious light. He shines from the world to come into the darkness of our days. This one " Image " renders powerless all the images of myth, but it also fulfils every true insight and longing which myth expressed.'

Oskar Simmel, S. J.

PREFACE

IN AN ARTICLE which has only come to my notice since the completion of this book Professor A. H. Armstrong uses some words which express so well my own thought about comparative religion that I cannot refrain from quoting them. He says:

> We Catholics are the very unworthy and inadequate custodians of the religion of all mankind, the servants of Christ the universal Word, who has always spoken to and acted on all men throughout human history, though generally secretly and obscurely, and by whom all that is good in human thought and practice, especially religious thought and practice, is caused and nourished: and he, and no one and nothing else, is our ground of security.
>
> (The Downside Review, April 1962. p. 111)

As Christians we should admire and delight in all that is good in all religions everywhere and at all times. We should look for good wherever we can find it in the religions of mankind, without being surprised if we also find a great deal of evil, for fallen intelligences both angelic and human have been at work to pervert and distort the truth. Few stories or 'cults' are wholly good or wholly evil; they usually contain both elements. Because we believe that Christianity has been revealed by God we can maintain a certain independence with regard to other religions, because we can test them by that touchstone which is Christ, the Incarnate Lord. This not only enables us to see where those other religions fall short of the fulness of truth and light, but also to trace those ways in which God has been touching the hearts and minds of men throughout the ages and drawing them to Himself.

I must here express my indebtedness to Professor Mircea Eliade of Chicago University in whose 'Symbolism of the Centre' the existence of a 'Nostalgia for Paradise' in the human race first came to my notice, and to whose other writings I owe so much. I should also like to thank Professor S. H. Hooke, Baroness de Ward and the Central County Library in Winchester for so kindly providing me with the books without which this one could not have been written.

My acknowledgements go to Messrs Sheed and Ward for permission to use the quotations from Father O. Simmel, S.J. in *Selection II*; and to all the other authors and their publishers to whose works I have made reference.

Finally I must express my gratitude to Canon H. A. Blair and Mr. G. C. Darton, both for their kind interest and encouragement and for reading the typescript and making valuable suggestions and criticisms.

+ *S. M.*

Wantage, 21st February 1964.

THE NOSTALGIA FOR PARADISE

INTRODUCTION

In the nineteenth century scientific research was regarded as a threat to religious belief— the two were thought to be incompatible.   To a very great extent this is no longer the case, and in this exciting age in which we live—the mid-twentieth century— it is becoming increasingly evident that a deep truth lay behind the words of Pope Pius XII, addressed to a scientific gathering in 1951, in which he declared that God was waiting behind every door that science opened. Père Teilhard de Chardin, in books which are now appearing in English translations and are fast becoming widely known, devoted years of his life to the elucidation of this fact in the field of biological science, or perhaps, more correctly, to palæontology.   There are many other methods of research which are throwing fresh light on the life of man, on his thought and his aspirations, revealing the profound meanings underlying the innumerable different manifestations and expressions of the human mind and thought.   They are revealing vast new perspectives and fresh evaluations of the various religious strivings of man.   It is true that this study is also showing ever more clearly how difficult it is for those brought up in one specific religious tradition to understand the true meaning of other and alien cultures, yet this is something that Christianity has always known, for Jesus Himself said that only by doing the will of God as taught by Him could we come to know the truth of his teaching.   Religion is, fundamentally, something far too intimate and interior to the heart and soul of man for its deeper meaning to be understood through doctrines and rites, however important and illuminating these may be.   If this is true of the different

religious traditions of our own day, it is probably equally true
of the religions of a bygone age. We have, nevertheless,

> a host of fresh insights by which centuries of prejudice are
> slowly being removed. [1]

The impression we now have is one of awe in the presence of
the vast wealth of religions and the many-sidedness of religious
phenomena.

Many years ago Professor A. B. Davidson pointed out that
the prophet Isaiah appears to have thought that God's purpose
of salvation preceded that of creation (Is. 45: 22). For the
prophet the purpose of salvation was not one *formed* by God;
it is rather the expression of His very Being, it is His
characteristic as God. Though it appears to us that this His
purpose was long delayed, yet it was finally executed in His
self-revelation in His Son Jesus Christ. It was necessary
first to reveal the goodness of His purpose

> because only through the intelligent and spiritual co-operation
> of man could this be carried out. [2]

There is something in man— and to a certain extent in
all living things— which responds to the 'holy' as to something
irresistible. It must have been this impact of 'holiness' which
first elicited the response of his disciples to Jesus Christ,
this that drew from St. Paul his passionate devotion to his
Lord. The response aroused by St. Francis in his followers,
as well as in the lower creation, again testifies to this power
of holiness, which men and birds and beasts find so attractive.

We can never compass the Infinite, and we must accept
this limitation of our 'creatureliness', but through all time and
eternity we shall be penetrating ever more deeply into it.
This is the wonder of life— its supreme mystery— and we
fail in that which is of ultimate importance if we allow ourselves
to become earthbound, caught up in the meshes of daily life

---

[1] F. Heiler in *History of Religions* (ed. M. Eliade), p. 137.
[2] A. B. Davidson *The Theology of the Old Testament*, p. 177.

so that the things which are of supreme importance and eternal value fail to interest us. In the following pages we will suggest some lines of thought on a subject which may be extended almost indefinitely, in the hope that it may lead others to read and think around this fascinating subject. It is, in fact, an almost inexhaustible theme in which we are only at the beginning of things, so vast is the field it opens up to our gaze.

Since 1933 scholars have met each year at Ancona in Switzerland to discuss these problems in the light of their various specialized methods of approach, in order to seek a clearer understanding 'of the world's poetic and religious visions, modes and dreams of life' so that these may afford us some conception of the 'manifold yet unitary past and also the present spiritual wealth which still lies untapped and unutilised in modern life'. Those working in highly specialized fields of study have come together to lay their findings at the disposal of specialists in various other fields. Here the history of religions, ethnology, palæontology and orientalism have come to be seen as capable of revealing human situations which are of value not only to sociologists, but also to philosophers and theologians. Thus the West has gradually come to know more about the fabulous and eccentric cultures of Asia, and ethnologists have discovered strange spiritual worlds which appear to be far removed from our modern Western ideas. Above all depth psychology has revealed vast unknown territories. Professor Eliade compares the discovery of the 'unconscious' with the maritime discoveries of the Renaissance and the astronomical discoveries of the telescope. They are alike in that each of these revealed a world which till then had been unsuspected: it was a kind of 'break through the planes' because it shattered the hitherto accepted ideas of the Cosmos, revealing unimagined structures in the Universe. [3]

When Jung revealed the fact that there was a 'collective unconscious', myths, images and symbols took on a fresh

[3] Eranos Yearbook IV. *Spiritual Disciplines*, Introduction.

significance. The explorations of the treasures of archaic society began to reveal much of the workings of the human spirit through the ages. Scholars dived into these ancient treasures just as divers descend to the depths of the sea, or explorers to the bottom of caves, to seek for material to aid them in their research. Primitive modes of psychic life buried in the darkness of the unconscious have become accessible to study through the work of depth-psychologists, and religious historians have realised that their findings are of inestimable value to them. Their combined aim is to contribute to the more perfect knowledge of the deeps of the human spirit. Even the strangest forms of behaviour and belief must now be regarded as a human phenomenon, of interest for its own sake, as shedding light on the deeply varied and extraordinarily rich content of the human person. To the scholars of the nineteenth century such an approach would have seemed utterly absurd, since for them savagery could only express a non-cultural form of human existence, and was therefore of practically no interest. If now the simplest 'myth' can be of real value and interest and be considered worthy of study, this must naturally apply in a far greater degree to the mystics and contemplatives of all ages. The study of various forms of mysticism, of the varied concepts of that unknown world which surrounds us on all sides, reveals a dimension in human nature which has almost escaped modern human society, or has been completely distorted by it. In our highly organized and comfortable modern life with all its technical devices which are now taken for granted we are no longer aware of those spiritual forces, both good and evil, which the primitives could not forget or ignore. Yet in many ways Christian mysticism comes very near to that of the primitive cultures. Possibly this is because in those early ventures of the spirit, in its simplest forms, we find something of the directness and awareness of the spiritual world which Christ revealed to us in all its truth and beauty.

CHAPTER I

THE NOSTALGIA FOR PARADISE

IT IS POSSIBLE that later ages will look back to this twentieth century in which we live as being characterized, among its many other achievements, by the discovery of the value and meaning of myth, image and symbol. The ideas underlying all the different religious cultures of the history, and even the pre-history, of the human race have been widely illuminated and enriched by modern scientific research into the supremely interesting reaches of the human mind at the various stages of its progress. It is now possible to discern in some measure what lay behind ancient myth and cult, and what still lies behind ideas and symbols in cultures other than our own. The idea of an original, perfect time before the Fall of man is extremely widespread. There are many images of a mythical event which led to the present 'fallen' condition of our race— a condition which appears everywhere to be taken for granted, whatever its cause. In other words, the *essential* condition of man— the condition in which he should still find himself had all gone as it should have done— is thought to have preceded the *actual* condition of mankind. In the ancient myths this decisive event which put all things out of joint, as it were, took place before us: it was caused by our first ancestor. Everywhere, too, we find the longing to return to that idyllic state, that is, to Paradise. In the archaic cults the original, mythical events which had to do with man and his origin have always to be remembered— relived— made present. This is what took place in the cultic ritual of the Ancient Near East, as it still does in varying degrees in many 'primitive' cultures of our own day, and, in fact, in the liturgies of the Jewish and Christian religions. Modern psychoanalysis has rediscovered this idea, with its theory that a patient must go over in his mind the happenings and thoughts of his past life, from earliest youth, in order to face and to 'relive' whatever may have caused the special crisis or difficulty in his life, in order to discern where his life became wrongly orientated and what it was that brought about his present suffering.

The perceptions of primitive man may seem to us in many ways crude and even childish, at least in the form in which they were expressed. A century ago our forbears spoke quite naturally of 'the heathen bowing down to wood and stone', though now, in the light of recent research, it is not possible to hold this attitude without grave reservations. When we say that the Catholic Faith is that which has been believed everywhere and at all times we must not narrow this down to some very definite doctrines, but make it as wide as we possibly can. Many and varied paths prepared the way for Christ's coming— that 'Coming' which gathered up and fulfilled in itself all those partial glimpses of truth and reality which had come into the hearts and minds of men through the ages. God knows and has known all things from the very foundation of the world, and man slowly, gradually, gains glimpses here and there of the divine riches. Even now all the extraordinary scientific discoveries of our age simply mean that man has gained one more insight into that which has always been there 'in God', waiting for man to see and understand. Mythical thought does help us to see the work of Christ in a new light, showing that it is the fulfilment not only of the religion of the Old Testament, but also of natural religion. Myths reveal some of the psychological roots in our human nature with which Christianity can deal so effectively. If, as we believe, Christ is the 'Centre' of all reality, or, as Père Teilhard de Chardin would have said, 'Omega point', the *end* of all things, then our investigations must lead us again and again to Him, whether we think of that vital theme in ancient thought, the 'Centre of the world', or of the 'axis' around which all revolves, of the 'Tree of Life' or of the Water of Life, of the 'ladder between earth and heaven', or of the promised land 'flowing with milk and honey'.

Ultimately all religion is based on experience. We can know nothing of God apart from the knowledge of Himself which, through the ages, He has been able to impart to us. Myths are open to scientific explanation. The recurrence of ancient and widespread mythical ideas in the imagery of dreams, and even in the delusions of the insane, points to something deeply rooted in human nature. They are related to universally desired satisfactions, and are found at all religious and cultural levels. The primitive formation of myths, however unreal they may seem to us, represent enduring psychological factors which have to be included in any live and balanced religion. For the primitives the 'myth' expressed *reality*: that which was *absolutely* true. It brought them out of the sphere of 'profane' time, out of the ebb and flow of daily life, into the 'Sacred Great Time', or, as we now say, into Eternity: that place where there is no passing time, as we know it, and which is always there in the background of all this 'passing show'.

The religion of the Old Testament, though it includes mythical passages and though its ideas are at times expressed in mythical terms, is pre-eminently *non*-mythical: it cuts right across the whole pattern of natural and mythical religions by being based on the saving acts of God in history. Only as it proclaims the faith in the One True God— Yahweh— and in His religion, which is strictly monotheistic and ethical, does the religion of the Hebrews become the most perfect and adequate basis for the Incarnation, and the perfect self-revelation of God in 'His beloved Son'. The central insights about God were, however, arrived at by certain other religious leaders of that period, such as Zoroaster (e. g. 1000-600 B. C.). The Hebrews gained their confidence in Yahweh by trusting His providence and finding it did not eventually fail them, however bitter some of their experiences might be. They saw the interplay of events and images as revealing the power of their God. We see the very centre and culmination of all in the saving work of Christ. He is *in Himself* the primary image pointing beyond Himself in His Incarnate Life, to God, the Blessed Trinity. Yet we must remember that no religion can be based purely on historic and contingent events: there must also be the 'non-historic' side, that which deals with what we may call man's *essential* condition, his position in the cosmos here and now and at all time, his impulses, his needs, his desires, in a word, his innermost self. 'God' said Eckhart, 'is the wheel rolling out of itself, which, rolling on, not rolling back, realizes its first position again.' Rolling, that is, from within outwards in creation, in self-donation, in self-revelation, and then rolling inward again into His own divine Being, which has never yet for one instant ceased to be the whole of Himself. God, who is tremendous life and movement, pure 'action' as against 'activity', enters

> into the multiplicity of personal life and persons in whom the world and the multiplicity of the world is contained. [1]

Thus God, in Himself, is 'living process' not 'static being'. Dr. Otto maintains that in mysticism there are

> strong primal impulses working in the human soul, which, as such, are completely unaffected by differences of climate, of geographical position and of race. These show in their similarity an inner relationship of types of human experience and spiritual life which is truly astonishing... there are within mysticism many varieties of expression which are just as great as the variations in any other sphere of spiritual life. [2]

Christianity came into a world teeming with various religious ideas, many of which it has inherited, developed and spiritualized. These ideas prepared, in their different ways, for the coming of Christ, just as many streams and rivers flow into the great ocean which is prepared to receive them. These ancient religious traditions were many of them extremely old and very complex, and we must try to see in them some measure of the self-revelation of God as well as some measure of response to His search for the hearts and minds of

[1] R. Otto, *Mysticism, East and West*, p. 70.
[2] Ibid.

men. Depth-psychology and the history of religions between them are beginning to discern a pattern— surely a divine pattern— in all the complex structures of archaic religion. Just as in mythical thought the 'Great Sacred Time' is alone real, so in mythical geography there is that 'Sacred Space' which is *real* space— that space in which the 'sacred' or the 'holy' has manifested itself. In that sacred space there was direct contact between God and man. The idea of a 'Centre', a place where earth, heaven and hell meet, where contact is made between the planes of being, is extremely old and very widespread in Oriental civilizations. In Babylon there was a list of names for those centres, such as 'Link between Heaven and Earth'. These centres, however, also linked that spot on earth with hell, or the 'lower regions': that watery abyss which they thought had been there before the creation of the world, and on which the earth was thought to float. In much ancient thought any oriental city stood at the 'centre' of the world, and was the 'gate of the gods', where the gods came to earth.

These two concepts of 'Sacred Time' and 'Sacred Space' have led students of comparative religion to conclude that man cannot live except in a 'sacred place', in the utterly real or, in other words, in God Himself. Scholars have found, too, in the long history of religions, two distinctive trends which are everywhere evident. There is the *easy* way of coming to this reality, the way which finds this 'centre' everywhere, in every church or temple, in every dwelling-place, for there is no limit to the times and places in which God may manifest Himself and speak to a soul. The second way emphasizes the *difficulty* of attaining to this centre and to union with God. From the fact that the simple, easy tradition is the more widespread Professor Eliade draws the conclusion that it calls attention to something in the human condition which he calls a 'Nostalgia for Paradise', by which he means that there is in man the desire to find himself always, and without effort, at the centre of the world. A whole array of myths, symbols and rituals point to the difficulty of attaining to this Centre, while another vast array of myths insists that this

Centre is accessible. [3] The desire to return to that time 'which was *in the beginning*' is very widespread, for even primitive man realised that the condition of this world with its conflicts and sin, its sense of separation from its Maker, was not his true condition: that he was meant for something different, for union with God.

This opens up many interesting lines of thought. In the following pages I will try to gather up some of the leading ideas in mythical thought in the earlier cultures, not excluding the 'primitive' communities which still exist in various parts of the world and which may be called 'archaic', which reveal man's innate longing for the 'paradisal' condition. We will also think of the early teaching of the Hebrew Scriptures, the Greek Mystery Religions, and the religions of the Far East, which are all 'religions of salvation', seeking to preserve something unspeakably precious which must not perish from this world and which is yet perpetually being threatened with extinction. We will endeavour to see, too, how in Christ all these deeper yearnings of the human spirit have found fulfilment. In fact, it is now being realised that Jesus Christ gathered up and fulfilled in Himself not only the many different concepts of the Old Testament and Jewish writings, but also other ideas and hopes and visions which did not actually enter, at least to any great extent, into Hebrew thought. This is, of course, a very wide field of enquiry, and here we can only touch on each point very briefly in the hope that it may lead others to pursue these enquiries further.

We will ask ourselves what such or such a myth or symbol reveals. What is it that these myths and symbols answer to that they have such a wide diffusion? Myths and rites and symbols disclose something man discovered in becoming conscious of his place in the universe. They reveal something of his deepest need, of his perpetual wonder. In the ancient world the myth alone was real in that it dealt with sacred, absolute reality, that which *was*. For this reason the various versions

[3] M. Eliade, *Images and Symbols*, p. 54.

of the myth of an original paradise, lost through some fault, are of immense importance, and they constantly recur. They reveal the fact that in the heart of man there is a perpetual 'nostalgia'. For what? For perfection? for peace? for happiness? or for union with the power that rules in the universe, for God? Does man really yearn to return to an idyllic state, some past 'garden of Paradise' and does he feel that this condition would satisfy the deepest cravings of his nature? Or is it something else that perpetually haunts his imagination, that leaves him unsatisfied with this contingent world and draws him out into the beyond?

It is of vital importance that we should ask ourselves these questions, for they most deeply affect each one of us. We will remember the Myth of the Fisher King, in which Parsifal's question, 'Where is the Grail?' in itself transforms everything, and brings it to life. The supreme question for us all is, 'Where is the supreme reality, the sacred, the centre of life and the source of immortality?' This myth teaches us that it is enough simply to raise these questions, to ask the central problem of the world, for the life of the cosmos to be for ever renewed: for death is often simply the result of our indifference to immortality.

The longing for Paradise is one that crops up again and again in the human race, taking many different forms, expressing itself in the various concepts of a 'Utopia', in a love for fresh beginnings in one way or another, or in thoughts of a place of perfect happiness, however that may be conceived. Even when these ideas appear on the surface to leave out all thought of God, as in modern Marxism and Communism, they still portray this desire for the perfect state which we may call 'Paradise', and which surely ultimately postulates an innate longing for God, for the 'Good'. Though our modern world is not rich in myths the 'mythical' longing for 'paradise' has never disappeared from man's consciousness and his desires. Mythical motifs appear constantly in our literature, though they have to a great extent changed their character. That which in ancient times was always connected with the 'sacred', has now been brought down to a secular, a 'profane' level, though the initial impulse remains the same. Modern man, where he has given up his religious faith and practice, betrays his innate desire to 'escape' from the deadening round of daily life by his love of entertainment and reading. There he is brought out, for the period in which the entertainment lasts, from the worries and difficulties of life, of the present, and escapes into a time that is, in some way, entirely different, though here it is usually 'secular' rather than 'sacred' time. The Christian is brought out of this 'profane time' and brought into the 'Great Sacred Time' of eternity during the time of the 'Christian Mysteries', in his worship and in the life of prayer. Popular novels and detective stories repeat the themes of myth and saga and folklore when they depict, as they constantly do, the struggle between good and evil, between the hero and the villain. The theatre, the cinema and television provide for the desire to escape from the present by providing distraction and amusement: for the time while they last those who watch are transported out of themselves into another time and place and form of thought.

No phenomenon of religion has been so universally shared by all the scattered members of the human race as mystical experience, however differently this experience may have been described. The sense of the 'wholly-other', of the 'numinous', only unfolds itself slowly and by degrees, as the created and limited apprehension of man can receive it. At first, inevitably, these 'touches' of God, His approach to the souls He had created to know Him and who were in His image and likeness, were largely unintelligible to those who experienced them. The first response to have been aroused in that 'religious moment' appears to have been 'daemonic dread'. At first it probably seemed to have nothing to do with religion, but was felt as something bizarre and incomprehensible. [4] The whole history of religion is the story of the gradually deepening apprehension of its meaning, and the gradual formulation of concepts with regard to that which is the True and the Holy. Mystical experience implies

[4] Cp. R. Otto, *Idea of the Holy*, p. 136.

a 'getting to the Centre of Life': to God Himself, to *absolute reality*. Professor Eliade has expressed the view that

> there is no break in continuity between the ideology of primitive mystical experience and the Judeo-Christian mysticism. Among primitives, as among Christian saints and theologians, mystical ecstasy is a return to paradise; that is, it is expressed in the annulment of Time and History (of the condition of the Fall), and a recovery of the situation of primordial man. [5]

This is probably very true, as far as it goes, but it seems to me that it is not the *whole* truth. Actually, this is the question we shall consider as we glance briefly in the following pages at the history of man's religious aspirations, regarded throughout from the point of view of union with God in the mystical life. This will lead us back to some of the very earliest records— records which modern archeological research has brought to light— right up to that most perfect and fully developed of all the varied forms of mysticism, which is that of Christianity: that Faith of ours which is still so comparatively young and which, in spite of persecution and disaffection still reveals a marvellous vitality and richness.

The memory of a 'lost paradise' has never ceased to haunt the minds of men, arousing in them a mysterious 'nostalgia', a longing for some perfection, some happiness, freedom and complete sense of well-being of which it feels itself to have been deprived. Throughout mythology and folklore, expressed in a vast variety of ways, this longing has persisted. There has also been the conviction that this blessed time would return: that there was some perfection of happiness still in store for man. The Greeks and Romans looked back to a Golden Age which would return once more. The Aztecs of Mexico believed that all their misfortunes were due to the fact that one of their gods had left them, but were also convinced that one day he would return and bring back the happiness of his time

---

[5] M. Eliade, *Myths, Dreams and Mysteries*, p. 70.

on earth. The Hindus of India believed that a small ship
Hinayana would bear man's soul away to eternal bliss, but
about the time of the Incarnation this belief changed into
that in a *big* ship— *Mahayana*. The individual soul would no
longer sail away alone in a small boat but would be carried away
in a big ship with the souls of many others and brought in
safety to the further shore, to Paradise.

There have been many expressions of this idea. The
Andaman Islanders believe that beneath the earth there is
a jungle in which the spirits of the departed live and hunt!
They conceive of a bridge between the earth and the sky
over which the souls of the just go to Paradise, while sinners
are relegated to a cold region called 'jereglar-mugu'. They
teach, however, that all souls will finally be reunited with
their spirits and will live permanently in a 'new earth', in the
prime of life, where sickness and death will be unknown.
Among primitive tribes in the Malay peninsular there is a
belief in retribution: the wicked are condemned to a miserable
existence, though sometimes, after purgation, they are admitted
to Paradise. For the just there is Paradise, which is situated
above the firmament and entered from the West: it is a kind of
glorified 'Avalon', an 'Island of fruits', from which all that
brings distress and suffering to mankind has been eliminated.
The tribes living on the banks of the Gariep have a myth of
Paradise called *Too-ga*, where all go after death, according to
Hastings while the Hottentots believed in a land above the
sky-vault where all goes on much as it does here on earth. [6] Their
divinity lives in a beautiful heaven, and the stars are the
eyes of sages and saints, the dead who have power on earth.
In Chile many tribes place Paradise across the sea, towards the
setting sun, and describe this Paradise in mythical terms
denoting the highest bliss. In South America the Puri Indians
placed Paradise in a pleasant wood full of sapucaja trees and
game, while the Eskimos of Greenland think of an underground
heaven, a wonderful place where it is always summer and
where there is perpetual sunshine, food and fruit in plenty: it

[6] Hastings, *Encyclopedia of Religion and Ethics*, art. Blest, abode of the.

is the destination of the virtuous, while the wicked are assigned to a cold region.

In Celtic thought the other world not only conferred immortality, but its good was wholly inexhaustible. The fruit of the trees in Elysium was the food of the gods, and when mortals partook of that fruit they, too, became immortal. This theme of immortality will be seen in most of the ancient myths— it is the most distinctive mark of the whole idea of 'Paradise'. We will try to trace the slow development of this concept which found expression so very early. The Celts placed great emphasis on the blessedness of Elysium: its music, its rest, its peace, its oblivion. Their idea of Paradise was much more spiritual than most others, and the thought that there the blessed dwell with divine beings brings out that longing for union with the divine which is the essence of all religion. The Irish Elysium was either beyond the seas or under the water, and often it was thought of as revealing itself suddenly on this earth as through a mist: a very Celtic strain. In Avalon there were no storms, no excessive heat or cold, no wild animals; it was blest with eternal Spring. There fruit and flowers were to be found that needed no care— a thought very characteristic of many conceptions of Paradise. It was the land of eternal youth. Everything there was beautiful, and, as in Elysium, there was marvellous music. In the early centuries of Christianity the thought persisted that Paradise was a place in this world, and even Christopher Columbus set out to find it. Many a voyage of discovery had Paradise as its object, and strangely enough, the journeys which were undertaken with that object were amazingly fruitful. Paradise in Christian thought was always placed in the East, in some faraway region beyond the ocean and the mountains. Possibly this idea was derived from the ancient myths.

This idea of an original Paradise— a 'time in the beginning' when all was ideally beautiful, and to which man longs to return, reveals the indestructibility of man's standards of truth and goodness and beauty. In some sense man feels an obligation to conform to that which is the highest and the best, and his failure thus to conform brings him a sense of the keenest pain.   Baron von Hügel once pointed out that

> if man's mind and soul can thus keenly suffer from the sense of the contingency and mutability of all things directly observed by it without and within, it must itself be, at least in part or potentially, outside of this flux which it so vividly apprehends as *not* Permanence, *not* Rest, *not* true life.   Let us overlook then and forgive the first tumultuous, childishly rude and clumsy... forms of apprehension of these great spiritual facts and laws. [7]

---

[7] F. von Hügel, *The Mystical Element in Religion, Vol. 2,* 1st ed., p. 193.

CHAPTER II

LIGHT AND DARKNESS

'IN THE BEGINNING God created the heaven and the earth'.
Here, in the first words of the Bible— the great 'Book' of
Jews and Christians and Mohammedans— the Priestly writer
proclaims his faith in the One God who by His power brought
everything into being; who spake the word and it was done.
When we consider the concepts of creation in the myths and
epics of the cultures which surrounded Israel on every side
we shall see the tremendous import of the proclamation.
This first chapter of Genesis, written somewhere about the
6th century B.C., is the result of centuries of Hebrew teaching
and doctrine. It does not set out to tell us *how* the world came
into being, but insists that it was their God— Yahweh— Lord
of heaven and earth, who created all things by His almighty
power. It shows us creation as standing, as it were, outside
God, over against Him, yet wholly dependent upon His word.
The next verse does, indeed, show some affinity with the
contemporary mythical thought:

The earth was without form and void, and darkness was
upon the face of the deep. And the spirit of God moved upon
the face of the waters. (Gen. 1: 2)

The idea that the world had its origin in chaos and darkness
was very widespread in the oriental world, and belonged to no
special tradition. Here, however, the 'chaos' may be taken
to refer to the process of creation, to the unfinished work
of God, though in much mythical thought it was something
that existed before God began His creative work of bringing
order out of chaos, which implies that God did not create
everything *ex nihilo*, out of nothing. We shall deal in another

place with some of the different conceptions of the origin of the world and the creation of man. Here we are thinking primarily of the teaching of the Bible, where the emphasis is upon the absolutely transcendent work of God, who created all things, showing that behind the blind forces of nature there was a *personal* God, by whom all things were made, and by whom all are preserved in being. After the insertion of this second verse, with its slightly different approach, comes the great assertion:

> God said, Let there be light; and there was light. And God saw the light that it was good: and God divided the light from the darkness. (Gen. 1: 3,4)

Before all else God created light, and He saw that it was good: 'light', indeed, is that without which there can be no life, and therefore it may be taken as synonymous with life. For the moment we shall leave aside all concern with myth and concentrate upon the meaning of 'light' in the Bible. The Fourth Gospel begins with almost the same words as the Book of Genesis:

> In the beginning was the Word, and the Word was with God, and the Word was God. The same was in the beginning with God. All things were made by him, and without him was not anything made that was made. In him was life, and the life was the light of men. And the light shineth in darkness; and the darkness comprehended it not. (Jn. 1: 1-5)

There is, however, one great difference between these two accounts. Genesis gives us the thought of the creation of physical, external light while St. John speaks of the interior life:

> In him was life; and the life was the light of men.
> That was the true light, which lighteth every man that cometh into the world. (Jn. 1: 4,9)

The light shines on in the darkness, and the darkness does not comprehend it. Because the life is light and truth it cannot be quenched: truth remains the truth, even when men cannot perceive it; darkness, being negative, cannot put out the Light. The Word, the 'light which lighteth every man' was at the creation, and without him nothing was made. Here, says Max Pulver, the Gospel speaks of

> The unrevealed, hidden God, before his self-unfolding in the Trinity or in the creation of the world.[1]

Yet the unrevealed Godhead already contained a differentiation of Being within Itself, 'The Word was with God, and the Word was God'. This Word, this Life, was to become the light of men. God, even in the original hiddenness of His Being, was not alone, in Him and with Him was the Word, who is the light and life of men.

Now, in addition to God— Word, light, life— there was a fourth entity: darkness, or the 'shadow' 'σκοτία'. This word contains many shades of meaning, such as night, blindness, impotence, concealment. We can bring all these meanings into this one word. The 'shadow' is something that resists the light, something on which the light cannot shine, and the brighter this light the deeper the shadow that is formed by that which resists it. Though this darkness is not able to quench the light neither can it apprehend it. To 'apprehend' suggests an independent force or power. On the other hand, we can also say that the darkness did not 'comprehend' the light, and this must be taken to refer to something personal, an active resistance to the light. Thus the opening verses of the Fourth Gospel speak of the still hidden Godhead before His self-expression and self-revelation in creation and the Incarnation:

> Of the first Thou, the Logos, within the Godhead, and of man for whom this Logos is both light and life. [2]

---

[1] Max Pulver, 'The Experience of Light in the Gospel of St. John, in the Corpus Hermeticum, in Gnosticism and in the Eastern Church', in Eranos Yearbook IV, *Spiritual Disciplines*, p. 239.
[2] Ibid, p. 240.

For us men light and life are the same.   St. Paul bids us

> Give thanks to the Father who has made you fit to share the
> heritage of God's people in the realm of light. (Col. 1: 12)

Further on in the same chapter of St. John's Gospel we
find these words with reference to St. John the Baptist: 'He
was not that Light, but was sent to bear witness of that Light.
That was the true Light which lighteth every man that cometh
into the world' (1: 8,9).   Here is the central thought of the
Fourth Gospel: He, Jesus, the Christ, the Logos, the Son of
Man, came to His own— not only mankind in general, who
are, nevertheless 'His own' in a very true sense— but also those
specially chosen and prepared through long centuries to
receive him, to 'comprehend', his chosen People, the Jews,
and 'they received him not'.   The 'true light' shines, but it
is necessary to apprehend and comprehend that light if men
are to become 'sons of God', if they are to be redeemed, for
this is no mere physical light which is open and apparent to the
naked eye, as is the light of the sun.   God still remains the
'hidden God'— hidden under the humble form of the Son
of Mary, veiled in flesh.   Yet to those who believe in His name,
that is, in Him, those who are 'born of God' (John 1:13)
He gives power to become the sons of God.   Though the
world knew Him not, yet there still remained, as in the whole
story of the Chosen People, a faithful remnant, who were both
able to apprehend and to comprehend in the truest sense.

The opening words of the Fourth Gospel do not refer to
'light' as an 'image' or a metaphor, or even as a symbolic
expression of the ineffable God, but simply to the inner process
of illumination: this 'light' gives insight and interior vision.
It is a process: there is nothing static about it.

> For God, who commanded the light to shine out of darkness,
> hath shined in our hearts to give the light of the knowledge
> of the glory of God in the face of Jesus Christ. (2 Cor. 4: 6)

Light is transfiguring.   Religious experience shines out in
the face of the saint: he is inwardly luminous.   Moses was thus

illuminated after his long sojourn on the Mount, and the people, when he came down, could not look upon his face unveiled, so great was its radiance. The conception of light in ancient Iranian thought came very close to that of Christianity, and it is perfectly possible that it formed part of the background of the thought of St. John. Among the Mandaeans baptism was performed in the Jordan, the river of light, and this may possibly be the reason why the Jordan, where Jesus was baptized, was chosen by the Baptist. If, as may well be the case, the writer of the Fourth Gospel was originally a disciple of St. John Baptist, the connection becomes closer and more probable. Father Jean de Menasce, O.P. has pointed out that the similarity between Christianity and Mazdaism consists 'in the common orientation towards 'light', considered primarily God.'

And in both religions men will enjoy this light at the end of a life which continues to be a struggle, but a struggle which is foreseen and sanctioned. [3]

In the early Church one of the names for baptism was 'φωτισμός' 'light'. It was a rite of illumination, because in it the catechumen was illuminated in spirit. The source of the application of φωτισμός' to baptism was probably the ninth chapter of St. John's Gospel, in which Jesus gave sight to the man born blind, but here it is taken to refer to an inner experience of illumination which is transfiguring, and in token of which the newly baptized were clothed in white garments. St. Justin spoke of baptism as a 'bath of illumination'. In Persian thought the pious man had a second, immaterial self which was the reflection of his luminous soul and, at the same time, his guide to heaven. In many different religious traditions the spiritual body is distinguished from the fleshly body. While the latter, the body of the flesh, is limited in space, the spiritual body can be extended far beyond the limits of the body. Even the Babylonian magi knew this.

[3] Jean de Menasce, O.P., 'The Mysteries and the Religion of Iran', Eranos Yearbook II, *The Mysteries*, p. 147.

The Fourth Gospel, therefore, makes use of religious ideas which were already in existence when it speaks of the light which illumines every man coming into the world, though the writer does not speak of a 'luminous self', as did the Persian tradition.   Nevertheless, we must not draw too sharp a distinction between the two views.   There are some recently discovered Manichaean fragments which speak of Jesus as the 'luminous self of the individual soul, and of all souls'.   Surely this is only another way of expressing the truth of the 'indwelling Christ'.

In this conception the nature of the soul is defined, it has a definite content, it is substantial, but not material...and the godhead is also substantial, it is light and life. [4]

We must conclude that light and life are attributes of the soul, which is by nature living and luminous.   According to the Hermetical writings man's central striving must be to return to his essence, to find his true self, and this knowledge leads him to know God and to be known of Him.   A prayer of Hermes runs:

'All our inwardness save, O Life, illuminate, O Light, spiritualize, O God.' [5]

A man thus filled with light returns to his profoundest, truest self.   This trend of religious thought was very prevalent at the time of the Incarnation.   In the Far East it has always been central, and has in many ways led to a knowledge of aspects of man's interior life which surpass that of the West, where the modern depth-psychology is beginning to explore the same ground.   Secret knowledge of God, gained in the interior life, often bestows supernatural powers.   We may think of St. Paul after his rapture, when he was 'caught up into Paradise', (2 Cor. 12:1-5) working miracles which testify to the authenticity of his mystical experience:

---

[4] M. Pulver, *op. cit.*, p. 243.
[5] *Corpus Hermeticum XIII*, 19, 7.

The marks of a true apostle were there, in the work I did
among you, which called for such constant fortitude, and was
attended by signs, marvels and miracles. (2 Cor. 12:12)

Though in Christianity it is held that all these 'supernatural'
experiences are not essential to union with God, which is
always a 'union of love', St. Paul's rapture shows that there
must always be a place for 'mystical experience' in Christianity.
By responding to God's grace the saints become God's instruments, and are able to express for others the divine revelation
they receive. [6]

The Christian Platonists of Alexandria in the 3rd century
called a man thus illuminated by God a 'gnostic'. This gnostic,
according to them, had found peace, he had become, as it
were, 'impassible'; he was a 'stander', a 'hestos'.   A later
mystic, Gerlac Petersen, in his 'Divine Soliloquies', expressed
this very vividly when he said that such a man was 'as a stone
that has been squared'.   In the familiar words of St. Paul,
he is 'rooted and grounded in love'.   For this 'gnostic' the
truth is not so much a fact, a statement, but 'even for the
gnostic who is not a Christian, it means a *person*'. [7]   The
Saviour is truth, His person is truth.   Not only in the words
He utters but *in Himself* He is the Truth.   It was this 'Truth'
that was 'made flesh and dwelt among us'.   When the Fourth
Gospel speaks of 'light' it refers to an inner experience of
reality, of truth.   The living thought and love of Christ *is* the
truth.   The 'truth' must be a Person, for the 'self' is personal,
and there can be nothing higher, nothing more perfectly
expressive of life and love, than that which is, in the fullest
sense, personal.   Clement of Alexandria insisted that even in
this life it is possible to receive the 'inaccessible light' within

---

[6] 'All contemplative souls have beheld an infinite light of the spirit, even
though they describe it in entirely different images and words... It is the 'light
which lighteth every man coming into the world'.   But despite this ultimate
inner unity, Christian mysticism overshadows non-Christian mysticism by its
scope, its richness and diversity.   If the cultivated world of to-day feels so strongly
attracted by Oriental mysticism, it is largely because the authentic tradition of
Christian mysticism has remained unknown.' (F. Heiler, 'Contemplation in
Christian Mysticism'. Eranos Yearbook IV, pp. 204, 5).

[7] M. Pulver, *op. cit.*, p. 251.

one's soul.   His 'gnostic' had gained this 'light inaccessible',
had grasped it by anticipation:

> For by going away to the Lord, for the love he bears Him,
> though his tabernacle be visible on earth, he does not withdraw
> himself from life. [8]

Thus, even in this life, he enters into the Kingdom of God.
Though Clement called this light 'inaccessible' his gnostic
had evidently attained to it, and the means of this attainment
was a discipline, both Christian and pre-Christian, to which
he does not give a name, but which may well have been the
source of Christian monasticism.   The ideal underlying this
discipline was the attainment of perfection.   Actually, the
monastic state may lead to illumination and rapture, but this
does not follow as a matter of course, for 'illumination' and
all forms of true mystical experience are a pure gift of God,
bestowed when and where He wills.   It is possible to prepare
oneself for this gratuitous gift by a life of devotion dedicated
to prayer and contemplation, a life which, in Christian terms,
is called 'the way of perfection'.   The true ideal of this life,
however, is not mystical illumination, but transformation
into the likeness of Christ in humility and love; that which
the aged St. John saw to be the one thing needful.

For the Christian the thought of illumination and light
immediately recalls the Transfiguration of Christ.   All
illumination and spiritual light are personal— the Light of
Christ, who is our life and our light.   This idea has been
much emphasized in the Christian East, where a special
method of attaining to this 'light of Christ' was introduced
at Mount Athos in the 13th century by a monk known as
Gregory of Sinai.   The movement then inaugurated— the
Hesychast movement— was one in which those who joined
it sought to live in silence and peace in order to be made
ready for the illumination of God, ready, that is, to hear
'the still, small voice', the gentle touch of God in the soul,

---

[8] Strom. 1, 24 & 163,4.

and to respond to it. At first this movement met with much opposition, though it was actually the revival of a very ancient tradition. The first form of monastic life in the Church was that of the Desert Fathers, whose lives made such an impression on the Christian world of the 3rd and 4th centuries. There are some things in the world of the spirit which crop up again and again in the history of the religions of men— something fundamental, something of the eternal values, which here and there are able to shine into the hearts of men and cannot be gainsaid. The Hesychasts saw the light on Mount Tabor as an *energy* of God, though not His *essence*, which they regarded as unattainable. This view led to controversies which we cannot here consider, but finally the Greek Church adopted their view, which is in keeping with the fundamental teaching of the Eastern Church that the Spirit of God is even now creative and active in the Church, as it was in the Apostolic Age. This doctrine of the 'divine light' is still held in the Eastern Church. In recent centuries the movement has received its greatest impetus on Mount Athos, where it was inaugurated. Russian spirituality has been much influenced by it, and a 'new Hesychast movement' has sprung from the Russian cloister of St. Panteleimon on Mount Athos. It inculcates the constant repetition of the divine Name— or that which is now so widely known as the 'Jesus' prayer. This invocation of the Name of Jesus, which in the West has long been associated with St. Bernard of Clairvaux and such hymns as 'Jesus the very thought of thee with sweetness fills my breast', which are attributed to him, may take many forms. In the East the commonest form is:

'Lord Jesus Christ, Son of God, have mercy upon me, a sinner'.

After long training the person participates with his whole being in this prayer, with every breath and with every heartbeat. It has its breathing regulations, like Yoga, and is thus brought into some affinity with the spirituality of the Far East. When the training has advanced sufficiently the divine Name appears inwardly with an all-embracing flame

and force. A saying of St. John Chrysostom is taken quite
literally:

> 'Preserve the name of God in your heart, that the heart may
> absorb God and God the heart.'

There is an intrinsic bond between the rich contemplative
traditions in Christianity and the mysticism of the East.
In the words of Dr. Heiler

> Despite all the differences between historical, eschatological
> Christianity and the ahistorical, acosmic religions of India,
> there is an ultimate unity [9].

The invocation of the Name of Jesus may be practised
anywhere and at any time, but preferably when alone and
quiet. The thought is concentrated not on the Name but
on Jesus Himself, while the Name is repeated quietly and
slowly. Then even sleep can be impregnated with the Name
and the memory of Jesus: 'I sleep, but my heart waketh'.
If this 'Jesus prayer' is used correctly the light that shone at
the Transfiguration of Christ will be kindled.   The Name
of God repeated incessantly at last becomes transformed
into the reality of God.   Apparently, even after many years
of Communism in Russia, as late as the Second World War,
and probably even now, many state officials in that country
belonged to this new Hesychast movement. It is interesting
to find much the same idea in other religious cultures, for in
the East the Buddha is said to be 'burning', and in Islam,
too, 'heat' and 'warmth' are a sign of union with the divine.
Light and heat are simply different aspects or descriptions
which run side by side in the writings of the mystics.
    In many cultures the symbol of the sun is the symbol of
the Godhead, for it is at rest, fastened as it were at the centre,
while the moon is perpetually changing, and is thus the
sun's opposite: its light is a borrowed light.   This idea of
opposition may be applied to everything: light and darkness,

[9] F. Heiler, *op. cit.*, p. 204.

height and depth, good and evil, heat and cold, male and female. It is known as 'polarity' and the deepest polarity is that between beginning and end, the first and the last. Christ is Alpha and Omega, the first and the last. One of the great symbols in alchemy was that of the union of opposites: it was its great mystery and ultimate goal. This brings us to the thought of darkness, the opposite of light.

Now darkness is penetrated and purified by light, but the light cannot be manifested without the darkness, which must, in a sense, be present in it. In Genesis we are told quite clearly that God made both day and night, light and darkness, and the psalmist cried:

'If I say, Surely the darkness shall cover me; even the night shall be light about me.
Yea, the darkness hideth not from thee: but the night shineth as the day: the darkness and the light are both alike to thee.'
(Psalm 139: 12. A.V.)

We must consider the night and the darkness in some of its other aspects, and not only as that which resists the light, or the divine self-revelation, but as that which, in a sense, makes it more possible.

There is no more perfect symbol than that of the 'starry night': only in the darkness of night do the stars shine out, and the more intense that darkness the more brightly do they shine. In Judeo-Christianity, the great historic faith, the night has been chosen again and again by God to perform His saving acts, when His eternal radiance and power shone forth into this world under cover of darkness. Truly could the prophet say 'Thou art a god that hidest thyself'. It was by night that the Israelites were brought in safety over the Red Sea, and were thus delivered out of captivity on the great night of the Exodus, which may be regarded as the very starting-point of their faith in God, when that which is known as 'Israel' in the world of the spirit— that tremendous influence in the spiritual life of the world— came into being. (M. Buber.) The Old Testament turns repeatedly to this saving act of God as to a great and most glorious deliverance, the

most perfect manifestation of the power of their God, Yahweh.
At the blessing of the New Fire during the Easter Vigil the
Church still sings

> 'This is the night in which thou of old didst lead our
> forefathers, the children of Israel, out of the land of Egypt
> dry-shod through the Red Sea.'

It was, traditionally, by night that 'the Word was made flesh
and dwelt among us', so at Christmas we sing

> 'While all things were in quiet silence, and night was in the
> midst of her swift course: thine Almighty Word, O Lord, leaped
> down from the throne of thy Majesty.'

Though we cannot really know the time when Jesus was
born it was characteristic of the Early Church to place this
divine birth at night, for the Fathers loved to dwell on the
thought of the 'hiddenness' of God, on His strong, sure,
quiet work. Certainly it was by night that Christ rose from
the dead, and God's saving power shone forth once more
into this world, for very early in the morning on that first Easter
Day, before the rising of the sun, the women came to the
sepulchre and found it empty.   Therefore in the Exultet on
Easter night we sing:

> 'This is the very night which delivers all who believe in Christ
> from worldly vice and from darkness of sin, which restores
> them to grace and makes them co-sharers with the saints.
> This is the night in which Christ burst the bonds of death and
> came forth as Conqueror from the grave... O blessed night,
> which alone merited to know the time and the hour when
> Christ rose from the dead!
> This is the night of which it is written: " The night shall be
> light as the day ", and " Then shall my night be turned to day,
> in my rejoicing ".   For the holiness of this night drives out
> wickedness and washes away guilt... It banishes enmities,
> establishes peace, and brings low the pride of tyrants...
> O truly blessed night, when Egypt was despoiled and Israel
> enriched!
> O night when heaven is wedded to earth, and God to man.'

The great Christian mystics tell us that in the dark night
of the spirit the light of God's grace shines into their hearts.
Our own mystical poet, Henry Vaughan, spoke of the night
as Christ's 'knocking-time'. Again and again in the night
of the most intense human suffering and pain the soul is
brought close to God, and is given an unshakable conviction
of His Love and tenderness.   There are many records of
spiritual experience during the sufferings of the last Great War
when men and women, both young and old, testified that
at the crucial moment, in the hour of their extremity, the
divine power made itself felt, upholding and sustaining them,
giving them a faith which could never again be shaken.

On Christmas Eve, 1513, a certain Fra Giovanni sent a
letter to the Contessina Allagia de la Aldobrandeschi in
Florence with a basket of fruit from the monastery garden:

> 'Would that peace could reach you through such things of
> earth,' he wrote, 'There is nothing I can give you that you have
> not got; but there is much, very much, that, while I cannot
> give it you, you can take.   No Heaven can come to us unless
> our hearts find rest in it to-day.   Take Heaven!   No peace lies
> in the future which is not hidden in this present little instant.
> Take Peace!
> The gloom of the world is but a shadow.   Behind it, yet within
> our reach, is joy.   There is glory and radiance in the darkness,
> could we but see; and to see, we have only to look.
> Life is so generous a giver, but we, judging its gifts by their
> covering, cast them away as ugly, or heavy or hard.   Remove
> the covering, and you will find beneath it a living splendour,
> woven of love, by wisdom, with power.   Everything we call a
> trial, a sorrow, or a duty; believe me, that angel's hand is
> there; the gift is there, and the wonder of an overshadowing
> Presence.
> Life is so full of meaning and purpose, so full of beauty—
> beneath its covering— that you will find that earth but cloaks
> your heaven.   Courage then to claim it, that is all... We are
> pilgrims together, wending, through unknown country, home.'

We, with the whole human race, as far back as we can go,
are 'pilgrims' wending our way, through unknown country,

to our home in God. Mystery still surrounds us on all sides
as it surrounded the earliest of men, in spite of the fact that
we are obtaining the mastery of space and gaining
vast insights into the workings of nature. In a sense, this
only increases the mystery instead of dispelling it: the mystery
of our own being, of man with all his mysterious powers.
In the following pages we will touch briefly on some of the
spiritual searchings of the human spirit in the history of man,
and we will seek to understand in some small measure the
fundamental longings of human hearts as they ponder on the
unknown mysteries amidst which they live, and upon the
supreme mystery of life itself, its purpose and its end. If the
history of salvation is as old as the history of mankind, if
God's purpose of salvation preceded His purpose of creation,
if the revelation of God in Christ is really the fulfilment of
time and history, then it must also be the fulfilment of all
religions. Then, too, the earlier stages of religion which
man passed through must have some positive relation to the
fulfilment in Christ. Somewhere, in the bedrock of our
religious consciousness, the religious experience and various
religious concepts of our primitive ancestors live on. In the
light of Christ it should be possible to look back and see,
even in the most primitive cultures, some flickering of that
light and life of God who made us in His own image and
likeness.

CHAPTER III

THE WORLD OF MYTH

THE HEBREWS LIVED as a small nation in the midst of
surrounding cultures which had their own very old religious
traditions— traditions which formed the background against
which the Old Testament was written.   In spite of the very
careful editing to which the Hebrew Scriptures were subjected
many strands of mythical thought, and even fragments of
myths, still remain embedded in the Bible— strands which
cannot be eliminated without impoverishing and narrowing
down that which it teaches.   The unique grandeur of the
prophets of the 8th and following centuries before Christ,
with their sublime proclamation of the holiness and love
of the God of Israel, is in no way marred by the fact that even
in the most beautiful of these writings, and in the very latest
of them, we still find mythical, lyrical language which
is closely akin to the spirit of the surrounding cultures
and expresses some of the distinctive aspects of contemporary
religious thought.   In fact, the mythical motifs in the Bible
are part and parcel of all religious thinking, of all the yearnings
of the human spirit, which are so deep and unfathomable,
so steeped in mystery, that only the poetic, imaginative
language of the myth can give it adequate expression.

The ancients, finding themselves surrounded by mysterious
forces which could at any moment shatter their lives, turned
quite naturally to their relations with those forces for the
formation of their myths.   Religion in some form is essential
to human life.   In every civilization, even in the most primitive,
there are traces of it, at least as far back as we can find any
records.   It is a characteristic trait of human existence which
distinguishes man from the animal creation.   Recent
discoveries have shown conclusively that wherever man

appears on this earth there God appears also. Research by
anthropologists among primitive peoples has shown this
conception of God all over the earth: the conception of a
Great, High God, the First and Mighty One. It is true
that this concept has often been vague and undeveloped,
rude and possibly childish, yet there it is. Many scholars
believe that monotheism actually preceded polytheism, but
since the Great High God was thought to be too remote and
too great to be really interested in the affairs of mankind,
the many gods of the various forms of polytheism gradually
replaced the One God in the religion and devotion of the
people. There is, however, an interesting point to be noted
in this connection. Though the worship of the people was
directed to their lesser and more dynamic deities they did in
case of extreme need turn their supplications for mercy to the
Great God, the Lord and Ruler of the universe. The traditions
we find in the Old Testament of One God under many different
names fit in perfectly with the results of modern excavations
and anthropological research.

Mythical thought expressed man's earliest strivings to
understand and interpret the mysterious world in which he
found himself placed. Nature, especially in wild and lonely
places, still brings the sense of mystery, of something 'far
more deeply interfused', which Wordsworth felt and sought
to express in his poems. In a well-known passage Charles
Kingsley, too, spoke of this feeling:

> When I walk in the fields I am oppressed now and then with
> the innate feeling that everything I see has a meaning,
> if I could but understand it. And this feeling of being
> surrounded with truths which I cannot grasp amounts to
> indescribable awe sometimes. [1]

This feeling of mystery comes to us often by the sea, in
a dark wood, on a wild moor, or before the grandeur of a
great mountain range. It is apparently much more clearly
felt in the less civilized parts of the world, and was probably

[1] Charles Kingsley's, *Life*, 1,55.

even more real to primitive peoples who lived so close to
nature and who thought of all things— trees and streams
and stars— as being inhabited by spirits or the souls of the
departed. The Book of Job speaks of the 'morning stars singing
together' (Job 38:7). Missionaries tell us that in places like
India, out in the wilds, the sense of a spirit world of good and
evil is much more easily realized than it can be in the midst of
our highly-mechanized and complex civilization. The
mythical mind apprehended a life-giving reality in the
powers of nature and in the supreme realities of life, such
as procreation, birth and death. The immense impression
all these facts of life and nature made on the primitive mind
is expressed in their myths.

> The myths told of saving divinities who became men; of man
> in his origin as a creature of light battling with darkness— of
> the dying and resurrection of a god; of heroes taken up into
> heaven, of a kingdom of the dead and of re-birth; of a new life
> and the final destruction of the world. Heaven, earth and
> the regions beneath the earth were in the myths a single unity.
> They formed the stage on which the drama of human life was
> enacted, where gods appeared, and good and evil spirits, and
> where miracles took place, relieving mortal men of their
> wretchedness. [2]

Naturally, the question arises as to the difference between
these myths and the Christian message. This was the question
that faced the early Church as it strove to bring the gospel
message to a world steeped in mythological ideas. The
early Fathers, in their struggles with the various forms of
gnosticism, dealt with this very question, and their answers
largely determined the whole shape of Christian teaching in
the West. The answer they finally gave was that Jesus Christ
was the fulfilment of myth because He Himself was not
'Mythos' but 'Logos', the very Word of God, by Whom all
things were made.
Myths cannot, of their very essence, be man's salvation,
because they are man-made, and man cannot save himself.

---

[2] O. Simmel, S.J., 'Myth and Gospel'. in *Selection II* (C. Hastings), p. 141.

Yet, as man strives to comprehend that which must always in great measure remain for him incomprehensible, since he is 'finite' and 'creaturely', and cannot therefore understand that which is Infinite and spiritual, he can only express that which he does apprehend in images and similes which are open to his sense-bound understanding. By the use of these he can give some shape to that which is essentially 'shapeless'. Of necessity, Holy Scripture, too, must employ symbols and mythical language if it is in some measure to make man able to comprehend the incomprehensible, for symbols are structural elements of our human nature, and are therefore accessible to us. In the inspired writings God uses symbols

> because He is speaking to man of His own reality, which is so bright and clear in itself that man can only see it through the transparency of images and symbols. Symbol in Scripture is God's expedient whereby He shows His glory to man. [3]

Jesus Christ Himself only spoke of our union with Him in likenesses and images. He is the Good Shepherd, and also the door of the fold by which alone the sheep may enter in; He is the Light of the World, which illumines every man coming into it; He is the Vine and we are the branches which, unless they abide in the Vine, are cut off and cast away and burned; He is the 'living water' of which, when men have drunk, they will thirst no more; He is the Way and the Truth— the Way without which there is no going to God, the Truth which alone brings us knowledge of God. He is the Bridegroom, whose presence brings perfect joy, and for whom His heavenly Father prepares the Messianic Feast, the heavenly Supper of the Lamb. It is He who stands knocking at the door of each human soul, seeking to enter in, in order that they may sup with Him and He with them.

The thought of the Old Testament, as of religion in general, is inconceivable apart from the language and concepts of mythical thought. The mythical passages in the Hebrew Scriptures are found not only in the early chapters of Genesis,

---

[3] Ibid., p. 156.

but also in some of the latest writings like those of the Deutero-Isaiah and Job. The third chapter of Habakkuk has a definite Canaanite background, and the triumphal procession of Yahweh in Deuteronomy 33: 2,3 is based on mythical ideas. The first eleven chapters of Genesis belong to the poetry of religious symbolism, not to history or geography. They deal with a different order of truth, with that *ultimate* truth which can only be grasped by the imagination and expressed in images and symbols. It is the truth of religious awareness, which deals with the relationship of men with God, who has made us in His own image. The relationship of the finite with the Infinite must always remain a mystery. This mystery is so vast and incomprehensible that only very slowly and stumblingly can even a portion of its truth be discovered by the limited human mind and heart. Again, though we have a share in all the various spiritual experience of past ages, and though we live in the light of the Incarnation, we have, each one of us, to come to the Truth ourselves, no one can do it for us. Myth, image and symbol have throughout man's history been the means of apprehending the truth in some measure, but ultimately it must be apprehended by the individual, personally, if he is to enter into the light. The forms in which varied insights have been expressed in the past may often seem unworthy and repulsive to later generations, yet in their measure they have done their appointed task of helping to bring man into touch with the divinity. When we speak of a 'Christian myth' we do not thereby detract from the historical value of the saving events from which Christianity sprang; we simply use the term to express the

ever-recurring repetition of a situation in which human need is met by the life-giving potency of a sacral act. It was the tremendous mystery of a dying and rising God, and of the daily and yearly repetition in ritual of the central situation which had power to meet every kind of human need, that made such an immense appeal to that world into which Christianity first entered. [4]

[4] S. H. Hooke, *The Labyrinth*, p. x.

St. Paul spoke of the 'incomprehensible riches of Christ', of His Love which 'passeth knowledge'.   St. John records the words of Jesus

I, if I be lifted up from the earth, will draw *all* men unto me.

The emphasis must be on the *all*.   Then we can see the prayer of the Muslim and the mystical disciplines of the Buddhist as part of the reaction of human souls to the magnetic love of God, manifested in the Christ— the Christ who was the Rock that followed the Hebrew Fathers in the wilderness, and who, though He may not be known to them as yet, is, we believe, perpetually drawing all souls into union with Himself who is their ultimate end and beatitude— Omega point— in which all creation will finally find its consummation and perfecting.   This thought may also be applied to all manifestations of religion, even in the earliest times and in the crudest forms, since Christ is declared to be that 'Word of God' by whom and for whom and in whom all things consist.

There is a sense in which religion means the search for the ultimate meaning of life and its goal, but this cannot exhaust its meaning, for it places all the emphasis on the 'human' side and neglects God's side.   The sense of the 'wholly-other', the *numinous* was at work in the very earliest stages of mythic experience, but this numinous only unfolds itself very slowly and by degrees as man is able to respond to its impact.   It was inevitable that at first, when man had as yet no spiritual data of experience to guide him, these 'touches' of God, His approach to the souls He had created to know Him, who were made 'in his image', should have been unintelligible to those who experienced them.   Possibly Dr. R. Otto was right when he said that in every case the first response aroused in this 'religious' moment in the human mind was one of daemonic dread.   At first it may have appeared as something that had nothing to do with religion, as something bizarre and incomprehensible.   The whole history of religion is the story of the gradually deepening apprehension of its meaning.   In the modern attempts to understand more fully the origin and meaning of myths and symbols a way is being opened up by which it may be possible to apprehend in some measure that which lay behind them.

The modern study of myth has revealed its close connection with the cult. In the drama of the cult an actuation of the original cosmic events takes place in which that which once occurred (or was thought to have occurred) is again realized, here and now. The myth was supposed to take place in non-temporal time: an instant without duration. It implied a break away from historical time into the 'Sacred Great Time', which we now call Eternity. The reality of the timeless, mythical event enters into the present moment. The participants in the cultic drama are loosed from all time sequence; everything is just as it was on the first day. Myth and cult thus create a connection between this world and the other, between the past and the present. A myth must contain a *basic truth*, something that actually has to do with the structure of being. Its essential truth lies in the fact that it embodies a situation of deep emotional significance. If the myth contains something which deals with human situations which constantly arise, and is able in these situations to satisfy the needs of men, then it calls for constant repetition in ritual and cult.

Another distinctive feature of mythical thought was that of the 'Urzeit-Endzeit' pattern, that is, that the end will be as the beginning— cyclic time. Though this thought is frequently found in the Old Testament in such ideas as that of the 'new creation' (Is. 65: 17); a 'new Paradise' (Amos 9: 13; Is. 11: 6); a 'new covenant' to be established (Jer. 31: 31), and so on, yet we do not find there the idea that there is nothing new, that everything repeats itself. The thought there is rather of a new reality coming into being through God's redemptive activity in history. In the Deutero-Isaiah, especially, the emphasis is on the fact that there will be something completely different and inconceivable:

Behold, the former things are come to pass, and new things do I declare. (42: 9)

I have shewed you new things from this time, even hidden
things, and thou didst not know them. They are created new,
and not from the beginning... lest thou shouldest say, 'Behold,
I knew them'. (48: 6-7)

The prophet looks forward to some future revelation,
something to which man by his own intellect and searching
could not attain: he will not be able to say 'Behold, I knew
them'. For Jeremiah the newness consists of the perfect
realization of God's original purpose:

This shall be the covenant that I will make with the house
of Israel; After those days, saith the Lord, I will put my law in
their inward parts, and write it in their hearts; and will be their
God, and they shall be my people... They shall all know me,
from the least of them to the greatest of them, saith the Lord:
for I will forgive their iniquity, and I will remember their sin
no more. (31: 33-34)

The Trito-Isaiah has the same thought:

Behold, I create new heavens and a new earth: and the former
shall not be remembered, nor come to mind. But ye shall be
glad and rejoice for ever in that which I create: for, behold, I
create Jerusalem a rejoicing, and her people a joy. And I will
rejoice in Jerusalem, and joy in my people. (Is. 65: 17-19)

Yet the new preserves the old: a new Jerusalem is to be the
centre of the world. Thus the 'Urzeit-Endzeit' pattern of
mythical thought is transformed. [5]
Though it is difficult to tell exactly what kind of religion
Abraham and his clan brought with them into Canaan, there
is a firm Hebrew tradition that for at least two generations they
had lived in a Babylonian environment before they emigrated
from Mesopotamia. In Joshua 24:2 a tradition is preserved
that Abraham's immediate ancestors 'beyond the river' in

[5] Actually the late Hellenistic writer of Ecclesiastes declares that 'That which
hath been is that which shall be... and there is no new thing under the sun'
(Ecc. 1: 9), but this is not in the straight line of Hebrew thought, and must not
be taken as characteristic of the Old Testament as a whole.

Mesopotamia, were polytheists, and 'served other gods'. Now Ur and Haran were centres of the cult of Sin, the moon-god. In this connection, therefore, since Abraham was able to obey the call of God and made that response of faith by which he obtained the divine promises, we will consider briefly this cult of a 'moon-god' and what it really implied. The cult of the moon is actually one of the leading motifs in mythical thought, and was widely prevalent in the ancient world. The moon, we must remember, was never adored for itself, but for what it revealed of the 'sacred', of *ultimate reality*. Primitive man realized that some strange power was centred in the moon: it manifested an inexhaustible life and vitality:

> The sacred reality of the moon was recognized either immediately, in the lunar hierophany itself, or in the forms created by that hierophany over the course of thousands of years— that is, in the representations to which it had given birth: personifications, symbols, and myths connected with *absolute reality*. [6]

Two leading ideas in Indian thought are that 'the moon is in the waters' and that 'rain comes from the moon'. All the moon divinities have more or less water attributes and functions. Certain American and Indian tribes to this day regard the moon, or the moon-god, as also the god of water. (i.e. Mexico and Iroquois). The ancient Greeks and Celts noticed the link between the moon and the tides, and from the earliest times it was recognized that rainfall followed the phases of the moon. The power to cause rainfall was attributed to many mythical characters. The Flood itself, which plays so great a part in much archaic thought, corresponded to the three days of darkness, or 'death' of the moon. Though this Flood was a great catastrophe it was, nevertheless, not a final one, since the 'new moon' again showed itself after the three days of darkness. Most of the deluge myths, therefore, record the survival of a single individual from whom the new

[6] M. Eliade, *Patterns in Comparative Religion*, 1958, p. 158.

race descended. Various reasons were given for this disaster among the primitives. In Australia there is a tradition that the moon one day asked man for some opossum skins to wear at night on account of the cold. Man refused, and to avenge itself the moon caused torrents of rain to fall and flood the whole area. In most narratives the catastrophes attributed to the moon were provoked by insults paid to it, or by the failure to observe some ritual prohibition, that is, by some ritual 'sin', which indicated that man was spiritually backsliding, abandoning law and order and thus putting the rhythm of nature out of joint. Connected with this, too, is the myth of regeneration: the appearance of the 'new moon' after the three days of darkness, fits in perfectly with the redemptive functions attributed to the moon and the waters.

The connection between the moon and rain and plant life was realized even before the development of agriculture. There is an Iranian text which speaks of plants growing by the warmth of the moon. Even to-day French peasants sow at the time of the new moon, while they pick their vegetables and prune their trees when the moon is on the wane, in order, presumably, not to go against the natural rhythm. Many of the fertility gods were moon divinities. Dionysus, for example, was both a god of vegetation and a moon god. The role of the moon in metaphysical thought was to *live* and yet to remain immortal, to undergo death, not as a conclusion, but only as a rest and regeneration. In all rites and myths and symbols this is the destiny man desires for himself. The moon, together with water and vegetation, has 'sacred value', and

> a sacred thing, whatever its form or substance, is sacred because it reveals or shares in *ultimate reality*. Every religious object is always an 'incarnation' of something, of the *sacred*. It incarnates it by the quality of its being, by its form (that is symbolically) or by a hierophany. [7]

Thus a *certain* stone, or place, or object is 'sanctified' or 'consecrated' by a ritual or by contact with a sacred person

[7] Ibid.

or object. The moon and water and vegetation revealed to primitive man an ultimate reality, a source of power and life from which all living things sprang. Man saw himself reflected in the life of the moon because of his own thirst for regeneration; his hopes of 'rebirth' gained confirmation from the fact that there is always a 'new moon'. Because of what happens to the moon, which is so closely connected with the earth, there is a 'life in death', and death is therefore not extinction but a change in man's level of existence. The death of man is not final because the moon's death is not final: it means rather another kind of life. In much early thought the moon was regarded as the land of the dead. The Elysian Fields, whither the great heroes were thought to go after death, were located in the moon. The 'Isles of the Blessed' were set in the sky, and all the mythical geography of death utilized the moon and the sun and the Milky Way. The moon's function was to receive and regenerate souls; from the very first it held some mysterious fascination and portent for man. Even to this day the Indians of California have a saying that

> As the moon dieth and cometh to life again, so we also, having to die, will rise again.

This saying is used in ceremonies performed at the new moon. [8]

For primitive tribes it is the regularity of nature, the continual repetition of the same events, that is cause for wonder. The ordered return of the planets and of seasons is the miracle that disturbs and affects them, filling them with gratitude and amazement. Miracle is the perpetual certainty of the order of creation rather than that which is unforeseen or unusual or unexpected. Giuseppe Tucci, in a recent book on Nepal, records that the religion of the 'Taru' tribe

> is the frank expression of the wonderment of a people thrust into the denseness of a hostile nature shoulder to shoulder with the beasts... Man has not yet risen to the consciousness of his own superiority over the animal world and has no

[8] J. G. Frazer, *The Belief in Immortality*, 1913, Vol. 1, p. 68.

advantage over it...the only defence available to man is
magic spells, incantations; offerings and prohibitions guide him
and protect him. [9]

At night these backward tribespeople meet to dance— their
only relaxation. This dancing takes place almost every
evening, but on special occasions, like the nights of the new
moon or the full moon, the whole village takes an active part
in the songs and dances, and they become no longer merely
an entertainment or a relaxation, but a rite.

What is it that the moon reveals to mankind? As we have
already seen, man perceived in the disappearance of the moon
and its reappearance after three days a hope of his own
regeneration. Therefore, the 'new man' survives the Flood,
as the 'new moon' survives the death of the old moon. From
this man dared to hope for his own resurrection after death.
The moon brings the thought of constant change, of the
opposition of light and darkness, of the full moon and the new
moon. The sun is the symbol of fixity, it *gives* the light while
the moon receives that light, and therefore its light is a borrowed
light. The moon thus symbolizes *receptivity* which is so necessary
for man if he is to apprehend the divine. The moon also
symbolises 'hiddenness': the dusky night, darkness, death,
seeds and larvae.

> The dominant idea is that of *rhythm* carried out by succession
> of contraries, of " becoming, life and death ". [10]

This 'becoming' cannot take place without drama and
pathos, and the lunar world is one of suffering and of 'history'.
It brings home the fact that nothing that happens under the
moon in this world can be eternal, for its law is one of becoming.
There is no final change, for every change is part of a cyclic
pattern. This idea of a *cyclic pattern* is characteristic of early
religious thought, and of all the fertility cults.

[9] Giuseppe Tucci, *Nepal, the Discovery of the Malli*, E. T. 1962, Unwin., p. 77.
[10] M. Eliade, op. cit., p. 182. ff.   See also the whole chapter on 'The Moon and
its Mystique', pp. 158-185.

In a sense it may be said that the moon reveals to man his true condition, that man sees himself, his own life's destiny, in the life of the moon. Therefore all moon symbolisms and mythology have something of pathos about them. In the most primitive stages of human life the myth of reintegration shows almost everywhere in the history of religion that there is in man a thirst to abolish all dualisms, and thus we may conclude that when man realized his place in the universe he desired passionately by some means or other, by religion or magic, to pass beyond the human status, that status which is so exactly reflected in that of the moon— and to attain to union with the power that ruled in the universe, where there would no longer be any possibility of change, no ebb and flow, but light and life everlasting. [11]

[11] Ibid., p. 185.

CHAPTER IV

MYTH AND CULT

THE STUDY OF ancient Near Eastern myths, which almost certainly formed the background of the Old Testament story of Paradise, has revealed not only a concept of an ideal Paradise which man hoped once more to regain, but also a 'longing for immortality', which may be regarded as in some way a parallel concept to the 'nostalgia for Paradise', of which, in fact, it forms one of the most distinctive traits. Man longed not only to live always in a 'sacred place', but also to live always in 'sacred time'— in Eternity. The myth was often re-enacted in the rite, and this rite brought man into that 'sacred time' for which he yearned. During the time of the 'cultic act', which was regarded as the re-enactment of the primeval events recorded in the myths, man was brought out of 'profane time', that is, out of historic time, and entered into the 'Sacred Great Time'— that which is always there behind the ebb and flow of earthly life. This did not mean that he wished to turn away from life on earth and to depreciate it, which is the basic longing lying behind many of the mystical traditions in the Far Eastern cultures. No, in those cultures which formed the environment of the Chosen People of God the myth and the cult reveal rather a longing for a 'concrete Paradise', which man believed might be achieved here and now, on this earth and at this present moment. Possibly the ancient myths and rites which were connected with sacred time and sacred space may be traced back to 'so many nostalgic memories of an earthly paradise' [1] and the idea of a realizable eternity, to which man thinks he may have access. The repetition of the archetypal events suggested the desire to attain to an ideal

[1] M. Eliade, *Patterns in Comparative Religion*, Sheed & Ward, 1958, p. 408.

from within the framework of human existence. Thus it is possible to trace a true line of development from these primitive conceptions right through the Old Testament to one of the ruling ideas of the Christianity of the twentieth century.

We saw in the last chapter the immense significance in very early thought of the waxing and waning of the moon, of its cyclic disappearance and of the ever renewed wonder of the 'new moon'. In this life of the moon man saw his own life reflected, and in the constant certainty of the appearance of the new moon after the three days of darkness he saw a hope that his death, too, would not be final. In none of the 'initiatory' deaths, or in the annual ritual death of the king in the New Year Festivals of the Ancient Near East, is the death something final: it is always an indispensable means of transition to another mode of being, a trial which is, as it were, the way to the new higher life, to regeneration. This same initiatory pattern is found throughout the history of religions: suffering, death and resurrection. Professor Eliade has pointed out that

> In the archaic societies man accorded such importance to death that it ceased to present itself as a *cessation*, and became a *rite of passage*. To the primitive man was for ever dying to what was not essential: to the profane life, and death came to be regarded as the beginning of a new spiritual experience. This was re-valorized in Christianity. It is the fundamental mystery: if one is continually dying to what is here below in order to be *reborn* to something else which is not of Earth but belongs to the *sacred*, then one is living a *beginning* of immortality, a growing more and more into immortality. Immortality is something one is constantly creating for oneself. [2]

Whether when we look at some of the early Near Eastern myths which have come to light as the result of recent research this can actually be borne out is possibly not quite as clear as Professor Eliade would have us believe, though

[2] M. Eliade, *Myths, Dreams and Mysteries*, Harvill Press, p. 227.

indeed, few are as competent to form a judgement on this matter as this very eminent authority on all primitive religions. What does clearly come to light is the longing of primitive man *at his best* for immortality, for a share in the life of the gods. We see man convinced that he has been placed at the summit of created life in this world, with a dim realization that in some way he has a 'share in divinity': that by origin he has in himself some affinity with the gods. Many Oriental writings express wonder at man's position in this world: a wonder that in our time can but increase as we see man propelling himself into outer space, trying to reach the other planets in the universe, making the most amazing discoveries, both in methods of healing the various ills from which mankind suffers and in methods of wholesale destruction of that life which he tries to preserve. A passage from an instruction to the Egyptian king Merikare from his father reveals this wonder, expressing the belief that man issues from the body of God, and is made in his image:

> He made Heaven and earth according to the desire of men, who are the " cattle of God ", and repelled the water-monster. He gave the breath of life to the nostrils of men; he made plants, animals, fowl and fish to feed them; he slew their enemies. He made the light of day according to the desire of men. He has erected a shrine around them, and when they weep He hears. . . the god knows every name. [3]

This passage contains the thought that all creation was solely for the sake of mankind, a thought which is also suggested in Genesis:

> And the Lord God said, It is not good that man should be alone; I will make an helpmeet for him. (Gen. 2: 18)

The Old Testament teaches that man should have dominion over the rest of creation:

> God created man in his own image, in the image of God created he him; male and female created he them. And God

[3] J. A. Wilson in *Ancient Near Eastern Texts*, ed. J. B. Pritchard, p. 417.

blessed them, and God said unto them, Be fruitful, and multiply, and replenish the earth, and subdue it; and have dominion over the fish of the sea, and over the fowl of the air, and over every living thing that moveth upon the earth (Gen. 1: 27-8).

Thus man is given a place between God and the rest of creation.

What is man, cries the psalmist, and the son of man that thou visitest him: For thou hast made him a little lower than the angels, and hast crowned him with glory and honour. Thou madest him to have dominion over the works of thy hands; thou hast put all things under his feet: all sheep and oxen, yea, and the beasts of the field; the fowl of the air, and the fish of the sea, and whatsoever passeth through the paths of the seas (Ps. 8: 4-8).

Besides the thought that man is made in the image of God, an idea common to Oriental thought, there was a tradition in some cultures that God formed man out of clay, and that human beings were created as a link in the re-arrangement of the world by the gods after the great fight between the gods in which, according to the famous Epic of Creation in Babylonia, Marduk killed Tiamat and subdued the other gods who had taken her part in the struggle. After this fight the world began to be created, and on Ea's advice Marduk created savage man out of the blood and bone of Kingu, whom Tiamat had placed on the throne, and who was chiefly responsible for the rebellion of the gods. Thus man was formed from the blood of a rebellious god, and this accounts for the two elements in him: the divine and the evil. In another Babylonian myth the thought is that man was formed out of clay mixed with the blood of a slain god. From ancient Egypt, from Assyria, Babylonia and Israel, therefore, came the idea that man was created in God's image, and in the pagan myths comes the thought that he was created partly from a god's blood. All these ideas suggest the realization in primitive man that he had kinship with the divine, that he could participate in holiness— or the divine life— which is an intensified spiritual power underlying all life. Man's superior position in the universe was due to his mental powers— his power of comprehension and of self-expression, by which he could show his wisdom, and in which he came very near to the gods themselves. Yet the gods, in ancient mythical thought, insisted on maintaining their superiority, while man craved for more than he already had. All these three cultures have narratives about the gods planning to exterminate human beings on account of their rebelliousness.

> And God saw that the wickedness of man was great in the earth, and that every imagination of the thoughts of his heart was only evil continually. And it repented the Lord that he had made man on the earth, and it grieved him at his heart...and the Lord said, I will destroy man whom I have created from the face of the earth; both man and beast and the creeping thing, and the fowls of the air, for it repenteth me that I have made them (Gen. 6: 5-7).

We must now turn to the myths which, with various other strands of tradition, formed the background of the paradise stories in Genesis 2 and 3. In these creation myths we do not find the thought that god created everything out of nothing— *ex nihilo*— but rather the idea of order brought out of chaos: a chaos which existed before the work of creation began. In the Sumerian version of the creation myth, which was probably pieced together from various other myths of origin, we gather that the goddess Nammu, whose name signifies 'sea' is looked upon as the 'Mother who gave birth to heaven and earth'. Other myths show that heaven and earth were originally conceived as a mountain whose base was the earth and whose summit was heaven. Heaven was personified as the god An, and earth as the goddess Ki, and from their union the air-god Enlil was begotten, who separated heaven and earth by air, and thus brought the universe into being in the form of heaven and earth separated by air. Sumerian mythology did not explain the origin of the sea. [4]   There are various myths

---

[4] S. H. Hooke, *Middle Eastern Myths*, Pelican Books, p. 24.

describing how the heavenly bodies and civilization in this world came into being. One of these is concerned with the moon-god, Nanna, or Sin. In this myth Enlil, the Sumerian high god, became enamoured of the goddess Ninlil and raped her as she was sailing on a stream. For this act Enlil was banished to the underworld, but Ninlil, who was great with child, refused to be left behind and insisted on following him. As this would have meant that her child Nanna, the moon-god, would be born in the underworld instead of becoming the light of the sky, Enlil devised some means by which Ninlil became the mother of the three deities of the underworld as substitutes for Nanna, who was then able to ascend to the heavens. This recently discovered myth gives a clue to something in the Tammuz-Ishtar myth, for in the Tammuz liturgies we find the names are frequently interchanged. The descent of Ishtar into the underworld, for which no reason is otherwise given, here finds an explanation. The moon-god Sin was the chief astral deity in Sumeria, and the sun-god Utu was regarded as her offspring, but in later Hebrew thought their positions were reversed, and the sun became the chief luminary. The Sumerians thought of their moon-god as journeying through the night-sky in a circular boat such as those used on the Euphrates, accompanied by stars and planets. Enlil was thought of as the source of vegetation, cattle, agricultural implements and the arts of civilization, though he used lesser gods to carry out his instructions.

The Sumerian and Babylonian creation myths reveal the fact that men thought they were created for the service of the gods: by tilling the ground for them they could save them from having to work for their livelihood. Enki was the god of wisdom, and under his instructions Nammu, the primeval ocean, and Ninmah, the goddess of birth, assisted by the other gods, mixed clay 'which is over the abyss' and created six different kinds of human beings. A further act of creation by Enki is also described: he created a human being feeble in mind and body, and then asked Ninmah to improve the miserable creature's condition, but she was unable to do anything, and only cursed Enki for making anything so miserable. This Sumerian myth may well have formed the basis of the Hebrew idea that man had failed to measure up to the place purposed for him in the divine plan of the universe.

In Babylonia the myth of creation assumed a place of central importance since it became associated with the great New Year Festival. This myth was embodied in liturgical form in the chant, known from its opening words as *Enuma Elish*— 'When on high'. Marduk is here the principal god. He defeats Tiamat and her rebel hosts and secures the seven tablets of destiny. He performed various creative acts. The seven tablets containing this myth were discovered by British excavators at Nineveh, and parts of them were translated and published by George Smith in 1876. Since then further portions of the tablets have been found, and now most scholars assign their date to the beginning of the second millenium, B.C. It is now known that at two points in the New Year Festival ritual the priests recited the *Enuma Elish*, with the force of magical incantation. The tablets begin with a description of the universe when nothing existed except Apsu, the sweet-water sea, and Tiamat, the salt-water ocean. From the union of these two the gods were brought into existence. The first pair were Lahmu and Lahamu (probably meaning 'the salt deposited at the junction of the sea and the rivers'), and they gave birth to Anshar and Kishar, which one scholar interprets as the circular horizon of the sky and earth. These in turn gave birth to Anu, the sky, and Ea, the earth and water god. Enki is here the god of wisdom, in place of the Enlil of Sumerian mythology: he is also the source of all magic. Ea then begot Marduk, who is the hero of the Babylonian myth. Before the birth of Marduk there was a conflict between the primeval gods. Tiamat made Kingu, her firstborn, leader of the attack, and invested him with the tablets of destiny. Eventually Marduk is enthroned as king on the other side and goes into battle against Tiamat, gains the victory over her and takes the tablets of destiny from Kingu, fastening them on his own breast. Marduk is represented as establishing the course of the year and the order of the months by the changes of the moon. The sixth tablet speaks of the creation of man for the service of the gods. Here Marduk, on Ea's advice, decides that Kingu must die in order that mankind may be fashioned. He is therefore slain, and mankind is created from his blood. The city of Babylon was built to celebrate the victory of Marduk, and a temple was raised in it as an abode for Marduk and his gods.

One of the ceremonies of the eleven-day New Year Festival took place on the fifth day, when the king entered this shrine of Marduk. All his kingly apparel was then taken from him and he was submitted to a ritual humiliation, during which he was struck on the cheek by the officiating priest and had his ear pulled. After this the king had to protest to Marduk that he had done nothing that was against the honour of the gods and the welfare of his state, upon which all his regalia were restored to him. Two other elements of this Festival were the death and resurrection of the god, as represented by the king, and the sacred marriage. This concept of kingship and all that it entailed was one of the most widespread in the ancient world, and cannot be confined to any particular civilization: it characterized man's thought at a particular stage of his development. In Mesopotamia it was an accepted fact that kingship came down from the gods, and the king, therefore, stood in a very special relationship to the gods: there was a link between the gods and the earthly king, who was their viceregent. The king was not considered as part of the community, he rather *embodied* it: he was in a different category from other mortals. One of his functions in all the Near Eastern cults was to offer sacrifice: it was part of his cultic duties.

Sacrifice has been found to have been one of the earliest religious acts. It probably originally took the form of human life, and though in Canaan and the Ancient Near East in general this was at a fairly early date replaced by animal sacrifices— the blood of the animal being regarded as a substitute for human blood— the original form continued in India till very recent times, and in fact still continues in the jungles of the equator. The primitive myth of 'a dreamlike age of the beginning, when there was neither death nor birth', but which was brought to an end when a murder was committed is widely known in the jungle villages of the equatorial zone, extending from Africa, through India to South East Asia, Oceania and Brazil. [5] The tradition is that the body of the victim was cut up and buried, and that from these buried parts arose the plant foods on which the community lived, while at the same time the organs of reproduction appeared in those who partook of these foods. Human sacrifices were made in Calcutta from all parts of India till 1835 A.D., when they were forbidden. A certain royal house in Assam had a custom of offering one human victim each year, and these victims were normally volunteers. One of their terrible goddesses was thought to be appeased by these offerings, and we read in the *Kalika Purana*, a Hindu scripture of about the tenth century A.D.

> By one human sacrifice with proper rites, the goddess remains gratified for a thousand years, and by the sacrifice of three men, one hundred thousand...Blood, if immediately consecrated, becomes ambrosia.

Though in Egypt the king was regarded as God, in Sumeria it was realised by about the middle of the third millenium, B.C. that man was not made to *be* god, but to serve him, to know and honour him. In Babylonia the king was God's 'tenant-farmer', the 'faithful shepherd', who cared for his people. The king's status was no longer one of identity with God, but of relationship with him, and in the course of the following centuries this sense of separation led to

> a counter-yearning for return— not to identity, for that was no longer possible of conception (creator and creature were not the same)— but to the presence and vision of the forfeited god... A progressive, temporally-orientated mythology arose, of a creation once for all, at the beginning of time, a subsequent fall, and a work of restoration still in progress. [6]

[5] J. Campbell, *The Masks of God*, Vol. II, p. 4. Secker & Warburg, 1962.
[6] Ibid. p. 7.

Another of the king's functions was to administer justice, as David and Solomon did publicly in the place of justice.

In Canaan and with the Hebrews this kingship belonged to God alone, and it possessed cosmic significance. When, in the 10th century B.C., King David wove together the Hebrew and Canaanite strands of culture the king probably still took part in the autumn New Year Festival at Jerusalem, at least in the pre-prophetic days. Many of the psalms are now thought to have been written in connection with this Festival. They are known as the 'royal psalms', psalm 68 especially giving a graphic description of the triumphant passage of the Davidic king to his temple. The relationship between the king and God— Yahweh— was of a most intimate kind. On important occasions the king led his people in prayer. This 'motif' of kingship runs like a thread through the long history of religions. When the Roman Empire, in which the place of the Caesars was of such paramount importance, finally broke up, the ritual which had for so long centred round the king came to centre round the figure of a Spiritual King, of him who gathered up in himself all these scattered fragments of ancient tradition which prepared the way for him in so many different ways. At the Incarnation the Son of God came to rule over the hearts of men everywhere, and to fulfil the deep, permanent longings of the human heart. He came to be not only the divine King, but also the good Shepherd, who gave his life for his sheep. Thus we may see a very real preparation for the Gospel in the pagan world, which was to find in it the answer to the religious searchings, and even the religious beliefs, of the time. Whether we see this as part of the deliberate divine plan or not, the preparation was certainly there, and the Gospel could not have won its way had it not found some echo in the religious yearnings of men's hearts. Though the ancient conception of divine kingship may be poles apart from that of Christ the King, since there is really no parallel between the pagan gods and the actual life and ministry recorded in the Gospels, yet the symbolism employed to give expression to the abstract yearnings of men has not changed: it has only become spiritualized and sublimated.

In the earliest culture pattern the king underwent a mimic death and resurrection to ensure the fruitfulness of the earth and the increase of men and beasts each year. There was, apparently, some kind of contest in which the King was slain and restored to life again, triumphant over his enemies. This was thought of as a re-enacting of the drama of creation, of the triumph of the powers of light over the forces of evil and darkness. A marriage typifying the union of earth and heaven frequently marked the victory. This feature of the New Year Festivals— the sacred marriage— was never lost in the Old Testament. It was something that the ancient kings could not neglect, since it belonged to the pattern of the sequence of festivals throughout the year. In the Old Testament, however, we find the distinctive concept of Israel as the Bride of Yahweh. Though Amos and Hosea condemned certain aspects of this cultus, yet Hosea, who was so strongly monotheistic, was responsible for bringing into consciousness the essentially nuptial character of the relationship between God and His people Israel. Here, at the beginning of the writing prophets, we find the marriage idea fully developed: Yahweh is the Divine Husband, Israel His bride:

> I will betroth thee unto me for ever; yea, I will betroth thee unto me in righteousness, and in judgment, and in loving-kindness, and in mercies. I will even betroth thee to me in faithfulness: and thou shalt know the LORD. (Hosea 2: 19-20)

This union is consummated in sacrifice, and the unfaithfulness of Israel is adultery and fornication. In Hosea the yearning love of God for His people is most tenderly portrayed. The early Christian Fathers often spoke of the Incarnation as the marriage of God with humanity: the fulfilment of the very ancient nuptial idea. In Exile this thought was developed to its fullest among the Hebrews: the sufferings they had to endure when they were stripped of all that had seemed to make life worth living, all that was most sacred and dear to them, did their appointed work of deepening their interior life and their faith in God, with the result that when they returned from Exile we find Israel for the first time idealized as the true Bride of Yahweh; her faithlessness falls into the background.   The prophet can now write:

> Thou shalt be called " My-delight-is-in-her"
> And thy land Married.
> For Yahweh delighteth in thee...and as the Bridegroom rejoiceth over the bride, so shall thy God rejoice over thee (Isaiah 62: 4, 5).

Other passages in the Old Testament also form part of the root of the nuptial Christology of the New Testament, though they originally celebrated human love and marriage.   Psalm 45 was a royal marriage ode, but it inevitably came to bear a more than human interpretation.   At first the role of 'Bridegroom' was assigned to Yahweh, but gradually it was transferred to the Messiah, the promised One.   The Song of Songs, which was actually only admitted to the Jewish Canon of Scripture comparatively late, clearly stems from the old Canaanite fertility cult tradition.   Professor T. J. Meek considered it to be a collection of fragments which originally belonged to the Tammuz liturgy, probably coming directly from Canaan, and certainly very old and archaic.   This book, despite its pagan origin, has yet adorned the whole conception of the nuptial idea in both Jewish and Christian thought, deeply influencing religious life and devotion. Rabbi Akiba (A.D. 50-132) interpreted it as speaking of the love of God for His spouse Israel, and spoke of this book as 'Of the holiest of the Holy; containing mysteries'.   The Mishnah also arrived at the view that, while all the writings are holy, the Song of Songs is Holy of Holies, and that the content of the poem indicates the relationship between God and His people Israel.   Later, in the Wisdom literature, Wisdom is regarded as the Divine Consort, but in Jewish tradition Israel herself has always remained the 'Bride of Yahweh'.

Israel was not chosen for herself, but that she might be the
means of God's self-revelation to the world. The very ancient
motif of the 'sacred marriage', so prominent in the fertility
rites, was taken up in the thought and teaching of the Chosen
People, and gradually sublimated and purified, till it was able
to find its perfect fulfilment in Christ. Though in the New
Testament the nuptial idea is not uppermost it does not
entirely fade away. The Bridegroom, who had been so
slowly and hiddenly coming into the world wherever it was
possible for man to respond to His inspirations and attraction,
has truly come, but the supreme 'mystery' cannot be
proclaimed to all; it comes out veiled, as it were, yet
nevertheless present. The children of the bridechamber
cannot fast while the Bridegroom is with them (St. Mark
2 : 19); the King makes a marriage supper for His son, to which
all are called (St. Matt. 22 : 2); in the Parable of the Ten
Virgins the Bridegroom comes at midnight (St. Matt. 25 : 5); and
finally the 'New Jerusalem' comes down from God as a 'bride
adorned for her husband', and a voice from heaven is heard
saying, 'Behold, the tabernacle of God is with men, and he
will dwell with them, and they shall be his people, and he
himself will be their God'. (Rev. 21 : 3) St. Paul saw the human
marriage relationship as an 'image' of the union of Christ
with His Church, and our union with God cannot be more
perfectly described than by the nuptial relationship, of which
it is the prototype. As Christians we believe that from all
eternity humanity was destined, as the Bride of Christ, to
share in the life of the Blessed Trinity, and that it was in order
to bring His Bride home that the Eternal Word became
incarnate that He might draw all men into the embrace of
His love.

CHAPTER V

THE SEARCH FOR IMMORTALITY

WE HAVE DEALT so far with one of the ancient types of myth: those which deal with the primeval events of creation. These, as we shall see, underlie in some measure both the accounts of creation in Genesis. There was, however, another type of myth with which these chapters are very closely connected: the 'paradise' myths. Here we can only deal with two of these, both of which reveal the search for immortality, which is one of the leading ideas in all conceptions of paradise: the famous Epic of Gilgamesh and the Adapa myth.

One of the most important figures in Accadian mythology is that of Gilgamesh, a semi-mythical king who reigned in Uruk for 120 years, and was the fifth king of that dynasty after the Flood. Being a king he was nearer divinity than other mortals, and it was said that he was two parts god and one part man. His mother was one of the lesser goddesses, and from her he inherited his great beauty, his strength and his restlessness, while from his father he inherited his mortality. The story of the Flood is now embedded in the Epic, though it probably did not originally appertain to it. Various fragments of this Epic, which was very popular and widespread in the Ancient Near East, have been found during recent excavations, and the whole has been pieced together in an English translation by N. K. Sanders (Penguin Classics, 1960). A very recent discovery has almost made it possible to prove that there actually was a king named Gilgamesh, and he may therefore have been a real prince whose exploits have come down to us in the form of a saga. Though he may not be the first human hero, he is the first tragic hero of whom anything is known. He is typical of the individual man in his search for life and for the understanding of its mysteries. Though this Epic was probably not written down till the first centuries of the second millenium, it must have existed in much the same form for centuries, and probably originated in the third millenium, B.C. The final recension was the work of Assurbanipal, the last great king of the Assyrian Empire. Amongst the texts

> Written down according to the original and collated in the palace of Assurbanipal, King of the World, King of Assyria

we find the poem which we now call the 'Epic of Gilgamesh' which still has power to move our hearts in this 20th century, for Gilgamesh at once enlists our sympathy. Some of the tablets were first discovered by a young Englishman, Austen Henry Layard, in the mid-nineteenth century. In 1888-9 an American expedition began work at Nippur, in southern Iraq. Among the thousands of tablets they found a small group of the oldest versions of the Gilgamesh cycle in Sumerian. Work there is still proceeding, and a joint expedition of the Oriental Institute of the University of Chicago and the University Museum of Pennsylvania has recently recovered some tablets dating from the end of the third millenium, B.C., one of which refers to Gilgamesh, though it has not yet been satisfactorily deciphered. It is, however, possible to say that this Epic was very widely distributed, and dates back to the preliterate age on the borderline of history and legend, a little after the great Deluge. The Sumerians were the first literate inhabitants of Mesopotamia, and the oldest Gilgamesh tablets are therefore in their language. In the ancient king-lists Gilgamesh followed a god on the throne.

The poem leaves us with the impression of a deep pessimism, which is probably true to the pervading thought of the Mesopotamia of that time, owing to the precariousness of life in the city-states, with their turbulent neighbours, and their recurring floods and droughts, quite apart from the vagaries of the gods on whom so much seemed to them to depend.

Though from the time of Hammurabi, early in the second millenium B.C., Marduk was the most popular deity among the Sumerians, he is never mentioned in this poem, which seems to point to a very early date for its origin. Here Anu, the sky-god, is the father of the gods, Ki the earth-goddess, and Enlil the air-god, who begot the moon Nanna, who in turn begot Utu or Shamash. In this poem it is actually Enlil who pronounces destinies as a sign of his supreme authority: he was 'power in action' while Anu was 'power in being'. In the great temple at Uruk, Ishtar, the queen of heaven, was worshipped— 'an awful and lovely goddess'. Ea, the god of wisdom, is also mentioned. In this Epic there is the constant sense of an underworld beneath the earth's surface but above the nether waters, the way to which was 'into the mountain'. It was, however, a 'road of no-return'. Throughout this poem the presence of the underworld can be felt: it is the foreseen end of his journey, though Gilgamesh tries so hard to escape it. Whereas the dying Egyptian of ancient days had a reasonable hope of going to 'Paradise' after the judgement, when the righteous man hoped to enter the fields of Paradise, for this

> rebirth was not for some exceptional man alone, nor for the king alone, but for " millions of millions...there is not one that fails to reach that place...as for the duration of life upon earth, it is a sort of dream; they say " Welcome, safe and sound " to him who reaches the West. "[1]

there was no such hope held out to the Babylonian. Among mortals only one had attained to that coveted place and lived for ever 'in the distance, at the mouth of the rivers', and who was translated to walk with God. This was a certain Utnapishtim who had lived in the dim past, and having survived the Flood had alone gained immortality. Here, as against most of the Flood stories, where one man survives to start a new generation of men, Utnapishtim joins the company of the immortals.

[1] N. K. Sanders. (English Version) 'The Epic of Gilgamesh' Penguin Classics. Introduction, p. 30.

Gilgamesh, realising himself to be superior to other men by reason of his great strength and beauty, could find no satisfaction for the cravings of his semi-divine nature. He had no equal until a wild giant, Enkidu, was found. The two became fast friends. At first they set out to win fame. Enlil, the father of the gods, had decreed the destiny of Gilgamesh, bidding him not to abuse his power and to deal justly with his servants, but Gilgamesh longed to establish his fame and turned his eyes to the 'Country of the living'. After many adventures Enkidu died, and Gilgamesh was heartbroken. His thought was now no longer connected with fame but with the longing to know the fate of his beloved companion, and the desire to find a means of escaping death for himself. He wept bitterly for Enkidu, and wandering in the wilderness he cried,

> How can I rest, how can I be at peace? Despair is in my heart. What my brother is now I shall be when I am dead. Because I am afraid of death I will go as best I can to find Utnapishtim whom they call the Faraway, for he has entered the assembly of the gods.

Now Utnapishtim, as we have seen, lived with the gods, in the land of Dilmun 'in the garden of the sun', and to him alone of men had immortality been given. On his way Gilgamesh came to a gate guarded by scorpions, who asked him why he had come on so great a journey, to which he answered

> For Enkidu; I loved him dearly, together we endured all kinds of hardships; on his account I have come, for the common lot of man has taken him. I have wept for him day and night, I would not give up his body for burial, I thought my friend would come back because of my weeping. Since he went my life is nothing; that is why I have travelled here in search of father Utnapishtim, for men say he has entered the assembly of the gods and has found everlasting life. I have a desire to question him concerning the living and the dead. [2]

[2] Ibid., p. 95.

The Man-Scorpion insisted that no man had ever gone into the mountain, for there were twelve leagues of darkness there, with no light whatsoever, yet when Gilgamesh showed his determination to go into the mountain, he opened the gate for him, wishing him good luck. As Gilgamesh went into the mountain the darkness encompassed him on all sides, he could see nothing ahead and nothing behind. At the end of eight leagues he gave a great cry because the darkness was so thick about him, but after nine leagues he felt the north wind blowing on his face, though the darkness was still as thick as ever. After ten leagues he sensed that the end was near, after eleven leagues the light of dawn appeared, and at the end of twelve leagues the sun streamed out, and he found himself in the 'garden of the gods'.

All around him stood bushes bearing gems. Seeing it he went down at once, for there was fruit of carnelian with the vine hanging from it, beautiful to look at; lapis lazuli leaves hung thick with fruit, sweet to see. For thorns and thistles there were haematite and rare stones, agate, and pearls from out of the sea. While Gilgamesh walked in the garden by the edge of the sea Shamash saw him, and he saw that he was dressed in the skins of animals and ate their flesh. He was distressed, and he spoke and said, 'No mortal man has gone this way before, nor will, as long as the winds drive over the sea'. And to Gilgamesh he said, 'You will never find the life for which you are searching'. Gilgamesh said to glorious Shamash, 'Now that I have toiled and strayed so far over the wilderness, am I to sleep, and let the earth cover my head for ever?' [3]

This is a typical mythological description of Paradise, or the 'garden of the gods', and we shall find some echoes of it even in the Old Testament.

Now beside the sea sat Siduri in a garden, with a golden bowl given her by the gods. She was veiled, but when she saw Gilgamesh coming towards her 'with the flesh of the gods in his body', but wearing skins and looking as if he had travelled far, she said to herself, 'Surely this is some felon;

[3] Ibid., p. 97.

where is he going now?' She then barred and bolted her
door against him, but Gilgamesh threw up his head and
lodged his foot in the gate, calling to her to know why she
thus barred her door against him, declaring that he could break
down her gate and her door, for he was Gilgamesh, the strong
and mighty one. Thereupon Siduri, having heard of his
prowess, asked him why he looked so starved, and why his
face was so drawn, as though there was despair in his heart, and
why he came wandering over the pastures in search of the
wind. He gave her the answer he had given to others,

> Enkidu, my brother, whom I loved, the end of mortality has
> overtaken him. . . but now, young woman, do not let me see the
> face of death which I dread so much. [4]

For answer she told him he would never find the life he was
seeking, for

> When the gods created man they allotted him death, but life
> they retained in their own keeping.

Gilgamesh declared that he would never rest, since Enkidu
whom he loved was dust. He begged her to tell him the way
to Utnapishtim, the son of Ubara-Tutu, saying that he would
cross the ocean if need be, or wander further in the wilderness.
Siduri told him to go down to the woods where he would find
Urshanabi, the ferry man of Utnapishtim, with whom are
the 'holy things, the things of stone'. Thereupon Gilgamesh
sped down to the water's edge, and when he found Urshanabi
he stood and looked him in the eye. Urshanabi said 'Tell
me your name? I am Urshanabi, the ferryman of Utnapishtim
the Faraway'. Hearing that he was Gilgamesh he asked
wonderingly why there was despair in his heart. 'I am
afraid of death' answered Gilgamesh, 'therefore, Urshanabi,
tell me which is the way to Utnapishtim? If it is possible I
will cross the waters of death'. Urshanabi bade him go to
the forest and cut down poles with his axe, one hundred and

---

[4] Ibid., p. 99.

twenty of them, sixty cubits long, paint them with bitumen, set them on ferrules, and bring them back. This Gilgamesh at once proceeded to do. These poles were to be used as punt poles, for Gilgamesh must not allow his hands to touch the waters of Death. He is to drop each pole as it reaches its full push. When he drops the last pole the boat has still not reached Dilmun, so he strips off his garment and holds it up as a sail, and so completes the journey; he

held up his arms for a mast and his covering for a sail.

So Urshanabi the ferryman brought Gilgamesh to Utnapishtim, who lived in Dilmun 'at the place of the sun's transit', to whom alone of mankind everlasting life had been given. Many centuries later the early Christian writers saw in the mast of a ship, with the sail hanging from it, a sign of the Cross of Christ.

When Gilgamesh at last appeared before Utnapishtim the latter looked at him and asked his name. On hearing that he was the great Gilgamesh, he again asked him the reason for his wanderings, and for the despair that was so clearly written on his face, receiving the same answer as before. Then Gilgamesh cried out

Oh, father Utnapishtim, you who have entered the assembly of the gods, I wish to question you concerning the living and the dead, how shall I find the life for which I am now searching?... Tell me, how was it that you came to enter the company of the gods and to possess everlasting life? [5]

Then Utnapishtim recounted to him the story of the Flood and his adventures, but added that if Gilgamesh wished to be tested he must prevail over sleep for six days and seven nights. No sooner, however, had he spoken these words than Gilgamesh, worn out with his wanderings, fell asleep. 'Look at him now' said Utnapishtim to his wife, 'the strong man who would have everlasting life, even now the mists of sleep

[5] Ibid., p. 104.

are drifting over him.' He then bade her bake bread, one loaf for each day, and place it beside the head of Gilgamesh, making a mark on the wall for each day that he slept. While the seventh loaf was still on the embers Utnapishtim touched him and he awoke, declaring he had only just fallen asleep. Then he was told to count the loaves and see how long he had actually slept. 'What shall I do, O Utnapishtim, where shall I go?' cried Gilgamesh. Then Utnapishtim told Urshanabi to take Gilgamesh and wash him thoroughly, throw away the skins in which he was clothed, and give him new garments to cover his nakedness— garments which would show no sign of age, but would always wear like new. He was also to put a fillet on his forehead, and let the beauty of his body be seen. Here again is there not some hint and prophecy of the white robes in which the newly-baptized were clothed after their baptism in the early days of the Church?

> So Urshanabi took Gilgamesh and led him to the washing-place, he washed his long hair as clean as snow in the water, he threw off his skins, which the sea carried away, and showed the beauty of his body. He renewed the fillet on his forehead, and to cover his nakedness gave him clothes which would show no sign of age, but would wear like a new garment till he reached his own city, and his journey was accomplished. [6]

Then, as Gilgamesh and Urshanabi were launching their boat, Utnapishtim revealed to him a secret thing, a mystery of the gods, and told him that there was a plant growing under the water, with a prickle like a rose or a thorn, which would wound his hands, but, if he succeeded in taking it, then his hands would hold that which 'restores his lost youth to a man'. Thereupon Gilgamesh opened the sluices so that the current of sweet water might bear him to the deepest channel, and tied heavy stones to his feet that they might drag him down to the water bed. There he found the plant growing, and though it pricked him he took it in his hands, and cut the stones from off his feet so that the sea carried him once more

[6] Ibid., p. 113.

to the shore. With joy he showed his precious plant to Urshanabi, and named it 'The Old Men are young again'. Then Gilgamesh returned by the gate through which he had come, and with Urshanabi as his companion travelled many leagues before stopping for the night. There Gilgamesh saw a pool of water and went down and bathed. Unfortunately, in the depths of that pool lay a serpent who sensed the sweetness of the flower, and rose up out of the water, snatched it away, and then returned immediately down the well. Seeing this Gilgamesh sat down and wept. Then, taking Urshanabi by the hand he cried:

O Urshanabi, was it for this that I toiled with my hands, was it for this that I wrung out my heart's blood? For myself I have gained nothing; not I, but the beast of the earth has the joy of it now. [7]

Thus Gilgamesh, the king, 'who knew the countries of the world', who was wise, who saw mysteries and secret things, brought to his people the tale of the days before the Flood, and engraved on a stone the whole story of his journeyings. He told of his single-hearted longing for everlasting life beyond the grave, and his search which disregarded all obstacles reminds one of the devotion of St. Paul, when he cries in the third chapter of Philippians:

I count all things but loss for the excellency of the knowledge of Christ Jesus my Lord; for whom I have suffered the loss of all things, and do count them but dung, that I may win Christ, and be found in him.

The lesson of the great and ancient Epic of Gilgamesh is that

even the man who attains the highest degree of wisdom and strength, thus obtaining the greatest share in the divine, is subject to the law of death. [8]

[7] Ibid., p. 114. (When the serpent steals the magic herb it enables him to cast his skin.)

Utnapishtim in this poem is another Noah, but it is not made clear how the human race continued after the Flood, for he himself became a god, whereas Noah was saved to become the founder of a new generation on the earth. The background, however, is the same in both places, for in this Epic we are told that the world teemed with people who multiplied and bellowed like wild bulls, arousing the great god by their noise. Then said Enlil to the gods in council: 'The uproar of mankind is intolerable and sleep is no longer possible by reason of the babel', whereupon the gods decided to send down the Deluge, of which Utnapishtim was warned by the god Ea in a dream. In Genesis 6 we find a small piece of undigested myth: the sons of the gods mixed with women, they demeaned themselves, and thus a generation arose which was so presumptuous that God could no longer tolerate them, but here the issue is purely a moral one, and Yahweh Himself is entirely in control.

The myth of Adapa deals with much the same theme as that of Gilgamesh. A fragment of this myth has been found among the Amarna archives in Egypt, which shows that it had a fairly wide diffusion. One Assyriologist, Ebeling, equates the name Adapa with that of Adam, and we may therefore consider this as a myth of the first man. Adapa was priest-king of Eridu (and some scholars stress the kingly aspect of Adam) the chief city of Babylonia. He had been created by Ea as the model man, but though he was given wisdom he was not given immortality. He had charge of the temple at Eridu, and it was his duty to provide fish for the table of the gods. Once, when he was fishing, a south wind suddenly came up over the calm waters and overturned his boat, so that Adapa fell into the water. Adapa, in a rage, cursed the south wind and broke its wing, so that it stopped blowing for seven days. When Anu, the high god, saw what was happening, he asked who it was that had broken the wing of the south wind, and gave orders for Adapa to be brought before him. Now the god Ea gave certain instructions to Adapa, whom he had created, saying that he must go with

⁸ J. Pedersen, 'Wisdom & Immortality' in 'Wisdom in Israel & the Ancient Near East', p. 241.

tousled hair and every sign of mourning, for at the gate of heaven he would meet the two gods Tammuz and Ningizzida, who would ask him what he wanted and the cause of his mourning. Thereupon he was to say that he mourned 'for the two gods who have disappeared from the land', and when they asked which two he must say 'Tammuz and Ningizzida'. Then, delighted to hear how much they were missed, these two gods would help him. All this came to pass as Ea had foretold, the two gods smiling at each other when they heard how greatly they were mourned. When eventually they brought Adapa into the presence of Anu the two gods spoke up for him and Anu was appeased, accepting the explanation about the south wind. Turning to the assembled gods he then enquired what they should do for Adapa, evidently with the intention of conferring eternal life upon him. He ordered bread of life and water of life to be placed before him. Now Ea had given further instructions to Adapa, warning him that he would be offered bread of death and water of death, and that he must refuse them. In accordance with these instructions Adapa now refused the bread and water set before him, though he accepted the garment offered to him and anointed himself with the oil they gave him. Anu laughed and asked why he had acted in such a strange manner as to refuse the food set before him by the gods. When Adapa explained that it was on the advice of Ea Anu told him that by this act he had deprived himself of immortality. The lesson contained in this myth is thus that even Ea, who had created him, tricked Adapa into refusing immortality, for had man been granted immortality as well as wisdom he would have been like to the gods in every way, and of this they did not approve, for they guarded jealously their own superior condition. Man, being close to immortality could not attain to it, for then he would have ceased to be human.

These ancient myths which have come down to us through thousands of years had their own part to play in preparing the way for Christ: they were surely part of God's uncovenanted mercies. They may also bring home to us with a startling freshness some of the precious basic truths of the Christian

Faith, of the 'Gospel' that 'good news' to which we have become so accustomed that we fail to realise how startling and how utterly satisfying are the promises and hopes held out in it to the human race. May we not see in this longing to share the life of the gods, this desire for immortality, some instinct implanted in the human heart which God wishes to satisfy? Just as the fact of 'conscience' has been taken by theologians and philosophers to point to the fact of a 'good' and 'holy' God, so may we not apply the same principle to all the other ways in which man through the ages, as far back as we can trace, has sought for God and for an understanding of those mysterious forces which he feels to be about him which he cannot comprehend. These myths may help to show us how the desire for everlasting life, for resurrection, for perfect freedom, is fulfilled in Christ, who came to set us free from the law of sin and death. Professor Eliade has shown that one of the great values of studying religions other than our own is that they help to throw fresh light upon our own Faith, to reveal the rich treasures of our inheritance. It is true that man still dies, but for the Christian the sting is taken out of death:

> O Death, where is thy sting? cried St. Paul, O grave where is thy victory?
> I am persuaded that neither death, nor life, nor angels, nor principalities, nor powers, nor things present, nor things to come, nor height, nor depth, nor any other creature, shall be able to separate us from the love of God which is in Christ Jesus our Lord. (Rom. 8:38-9)
> These things have I written, says St. John, that ye may believe on the name of the Son of God; that ye may know that ye have eternal life... We know that the Son of God is come, and hath given us an understanding, that we may know him that is true, and that we are in him that is true, even in his Son Jesus Christ. This is the true God, and eternal life. (1 Jn. 5:13, 20)

CHAPTER VI

THE GARDEN OF EDEN

ISRAEL DEVELOPED MOST of its mythology and its ritual on the pattern of the surrounding pagan cultures of the Ancient Near East. When the Hebrews entered into Canaan they took over the great centres of the Canaanite cult: Shechem, Bethel and Shiloh, and turned them into centres for the worship of their God— Yahweh. These places remained the centres of their seasonal festivals up to the time when Solomon made Jerusalem the chief national cult-centre. Instead of the myth celebrating Marduk's victory over the sea-dragon Tiamat they celebrated the deliverance of the Hebrew people out of Egypt, when God's hand had been so clearly visible. This Exodus formed, as it were, the very foundation of their faith in God. The great New Year Festival was continued under the Davidic kings for at least two centuries, that is, till the time of the eighth century prophets. In the Book of Exodus the Israelites are commanded to observe for ever the remembrance of their deliverance from the hand of Pharaoh, and when their children ask them, 'What mean ye by this service?', they shall answer:

> It is the sacrifice of the Lord's passover, who passed over the houses of the children of Israel in Egypt, when he smote the Egyptians, and delivered our houses (Ex. 12:27).

This thought often meets us again in the psalms, especially in psalm 136 where it is set out in antiphonal form:

> O give thanks unto the Lord; for he is good; and his mercy endureth for ever.
> O give thanks unto the God of all gods; for his mercy endureth for ever. . . .

Who only doeth great wonders; for his mercy endureth for ever.
Who by his excellent wisdom made the heavens; for his mercy endureth for ever.
Who laid out the earth above the waters; for his mercy endureth for ever.
Who hath made great lights: for his mercy endureth for ever.
Who smote Egypt with their first-born; for his mercy endureth for ever.
And brought out Israel from among them; for his mercy endureth for ever.
With a mighty hand and stretched out arm; for his mercy endureth for ever.
Who divided the Red Sea in two parts; for his mercy endureth for ever.
And made Israel to go through the midst of it; for his mercy endureth for ever.

Here this redeeming work of deliverance is brought into line with the original work of creation: both manifest the glory of God.

Psalm 78, too, recounts these saving acts of God:

Marvellous things did he in the sight of their fathers, in the land of Egypt, in the field of Zoan.
He divided the Red Sea in two parts, and caused them to pass through; and he made the waters to stand on an heap.
In the daytime also he led them with a cloud, and all night with the light of fire.

The second and third chapters of Genesis, which contain the biblical account of Paradise, are attributed to a writer designated as the 'Yahwist', who probably wrote about the year 950 B.C., in the David-Solomon era. They reveal the deep spiritual insight of the Hebrew people of that time— the time when many of the psalms were probably composed. Though no actual parallel can be found, the theme of the Garden of Eden is quite definitely taken from the creation myths of Babylonia and Mesopotamia, some of which we have been considering, though many traditions are woven together

in the biblical narrative. These chapters, however, are marked
by a sober simplicity which reveals the influence of the religion
of Abraham and Moses in its deepened spirituality and its
lack of exaggeration. It is interesting to compare the
description of Paradise in Genesis with the much later account
found in Ezekiel 28:13ff:

> Thou hast been in Eden the garden of God; every precious
> stone was thy covering, the sardius, topaz, and the diamond,
> the beryl, the onyx, and the jasper, the sapphire, the emerald,
> and the carbuncle, and gold: the workmanship of thy tabrets
> and of thy pipes was prepared in thee in the day that thou
> wast created.
> Thou art the anointed cherub that covereth; and I have set
> thee so; thou wast upon the holy mountain of God: thou hast
> walked up and down in the midst of the stones of fire.
> Thou wast perfect in thy ways from the day thou wast created,
> till iniquity was found in thee...
> Thine heart was lifted up because of thy beauty, thou hast
> corrupted thy wisdom by reason of thy brightness: I will cast
> thee to the ground.

This passage has far more of the fanciful mythical colouring
of the old pagan myths, lacking the limpid beauty of the
Yahwist's story. Yet, for some strange reason, it has almost
imperceptibly influenced Christian teaching on Paradise and
the Fall. Many of the ideas which we have seen in the old
'paradise' myths have crept into our thought on this subject.
In some of the ancient myths Paradise is regarded as the
abode of God himself, but in Genesis even the expression
'garden of God' is no longer used, though it re-appears in
Ezekiel, where this garden is situated on the 'holy mountain'
where dwelt a divine being, anointed by God:

> You were the signet of perfection, full of wisdom, and perfect
> in beauty. You were in Eden, the garden of God; every
> precious stone was your covering... On the day you were
> created they were prepared. With an anointed guardian
> angel I placed you; you were on the holy mountain of God...
> you were blameless in your ways... and you sinned; so I cast

you out as a profane thing from the mountain of God and the guardian cherub drove you out.   Your heart was proud because of your beauty (Ezek. 28:12-17 R.S.V.).

All this beauty was the cause of his fall, for his heart was lifted up and he was corrupted.   Pride led to his fall, and to his being cast out of the garden of God.

In many archaic cultures and mythical concepts Paradise is a place where no work at all has to be done, everything is provided: there are forests of trees laden with fruit, the mountains flow with honey, all work is performed automatically.   African myths relating to the 'paradise' epoch speak of the days when there was no such thing as death and when men knew nothing about it, of a time when they understood the language of animals and, living at peace with them, had domination over them.   They did no work in those wonderful far-off days *at the beginning*, but found plenty of food always within their reach.   Much the same concept is found all over the world, and all these concepts contain, as a *sine qua non*, the thought of immortality.   There are two main categories of these myths: those that speak of the close proximity between heaven and earth in primeval times, and those that refer to a concrete means of communication between them.   Heaven, *in that time*, is simply depicted as being very close to earth, or as being easily accessible either by climbing a tree or a tropical creeper or a ladder, or by scaling a mountain.   When heaven had become abruptly separated from earth, that is, when it had become as remote as it is now, when the tree connecting heaven and earth had been cut, the paradisal stage of man's life was over, and he entered his present condition, though still retaining a 'nostalgia' for the former state, which is conceived as man's *real* state: that which he would now be enjoying had the rupture between heaven and earth never taken place.   Man is shown, in these myths, to have enjoyed a beatitude characterized by freedom and spontaneity.   In those days the gods came to earth and mingled with men— the myth we still find embedded in Genesis 6— and man could quite easily climb up to heaven. Even among the most primitive tribes such as the Australian Pygmy and Arctic, there is an idea of an 'axis mundi', a 'centre of the world', connecting earth and heaven. By means of special techniques the 'shamans', that is, the 'mystics', among them try to rise above the present condition of man in his fallen state, and to re-enter the state described in their myths of Paradise. These 'shamans' are specialists in ecstasy, and during these ecstasies they pass out of the body and make the mystical journey through the cosmos. They are the spiritual directors of the people, for they are specialists in matters of the spirit, who understand most perfectly the souls of men. They are at the same time healers. In fact, they represent in the primitive societies the 'mystics' of the more highly developed religious cultures.

One strange method of attaining ecstasy employed by these 'shamans' is by imitating the cries and language of animals and birds in order to enter into that companionship with the animal world which is thought to have been one of the characteristics of the paradisal state— part, that is to say, of the perfect human condition. It must be remembered, however, that when the shamans utter these animal shrieks and cries which are meant to imitate the language of the lower creation, they only do so as a preparation for 'ecstasy': it is the pre-ecstatic state, the means by which they are taken out of the present condition in history and brought into that condition which prevailed before the Fall. A point of great interest lies in the fact that the heavenly ascension itself is contrived by means of a tree, or pillar, symbolizing the 'cosmic tree'. The Attaic shaman, for instance, uses a young birch tree stripped of its lower branches, on the trunk of which footholds have been made. It is a symbol of the Tree of the World, and the 7, 9 or 12 notches represent the corresponding number of heavens: the different celestial levels. During the initiation ceremony of certain other tribes a ritual post is set up which the initiate has to climb, and which represents the Cosmic Tree which is to be found at the *centre of the world*. On reaching the top the initiate utters a loud cry, invoking the help of the gods, since there, at the top of the post, he finds himself in their presence. Another tribe, the Koreaks, insist that they remember the time when their hero— Great Raven— went up to heaven without any difficulty. During his mystical journeys the shaman re-establishes the communication that once existed between heaven and earth: the 'paradisal state' exists for him for the short time of the ecstasy. [1]

Thus, clearly, the most typical experience of the archaic societies reveals a 'nostalgia for Paradise', a desire to recover the condition before the Fall, when men walked with their gods in familiar intercourse. A certain longing for Paradise appears at every level of human life— or 'religious' life— but above all it reveals itself in mystical experience. Among primitives, as among Christian mystics and theologians, mystical ecstasy is a return to Paradise. Professor Eliade sees in this a desire to recover the situation of primordial man— that time in which Time and History (and therefore the Fall) are annulled— and in this close connection between primitive types of mysticism and the Christian idea of Paradise he sees a clear ideological continuity: a link which appears to be lacking in the more highly developed religions of the East, such as those of India, China and Japan. At the very beginning of the religious history of the human race we find that same longing for Paradise which we find again in Christianity, the most recent and most highly developed mysticism. May we conclude from this that there is the remembrance in the 'collective unconscious', if we may employ that term, of a non-historical happiness which continues to haunt humanity, and which has never ceased to haunt man since he first became aware of his situation in the cosmos? [2] This 'nostalgia for Paradise' haunted Isaiah— that great mystic of the Old Testament— as well as Virgil; it nourished the saintliness of the Fathers of the Christian Church, and blossomed in the life of St Francis of Assisi and his early followers. Yet between this 'nostalgia' which is present in all the pagan cultures and

---

[1] For a development of this idea see M. Eliade, *Myths, Dreams* and *Mysteries*, Harvill Press, p. 71.
[2] Ibid.

that of Christianity we must be careful to draw a very clear distinction which is of vital importance, and which we hope to make clear in the course of our study. There can be no question that the 'nostalgia' is there, in the human heart and mind, but the question we would put to ourselves here is that of the *ultimate* source and cause of this nostalgic longing. What really lies behind it?

The myths of Paradise are among the most beautiful in existence, for they tell of Paradise and the Fall, by which man lost his communion with the gods, but which also left him with a persistent desire to re-establish that union which he had somehow lost. He felt a sense of frustration and unfulfilment. All the myths contain the motif of possible communication between heaven and earth, and they are all, therefore, of equal importance for the history of religions, for they are spiritual documents of great value, expressing the existential predicaments of man in this world, disclosing his obscure longings and desires. Each one must be taken to represent an authentic spiritual experience, in which human souls have been profoundly involved. There are many features common to all paradise myths. The savage as well as the European Christian thinks of a time when men enjoyed every beatitude, for perfection existed at the beginning. Both Paradise and perfection have in some way or other been lost, and man seeks to regain both the one and the other. Periodically, in the cult, the savage re-enacted the events that placed him in his 'fallen' condition, and this was, in a sense, a form of 'nostalgia'. Only to the mystics in every religious culture was it given to re-enter for a time the 'paradisal' existence, that is, for the time of their ecstasies. For the Christian Church, as for the primitive cultures, these ecstatic experiences, though they are not the lot of all, are of value for the whole community, for its ideas of God, of the soul, and of the spiritual life in general are derived from the mystics. This 'nostalgia' probably contributed in no small degree to the cultural creations of primitive man.

The first eleven chapters of Genesis do not deal with history or geography, they do not attempt to tell us *how* everything

came into being in the scientific sense. They belong rather
to the poetic and symbolic expression of religious *awareness*.
They deal with that *ultimate truth* which can only be grasped
by man's imagination and inner perception, and this must
be expressed in terms of images and symbols; for they speak of
the relationship of God with man, whom He has made in
His own image. The relationship of the finite with the
Infinite must always remain a mystery. In these earliest
chapters of the Bible many lines of thought and tradition are
gathered up, leaving us much to ponder. The account of the
creation in Genesis 1 must have been directed by an anti-
dramatic tendency, since for the writer Yahweh is not the
dragon-slayer, like Marduk in the early creation myth, but
solely the creator of the world. The Priestly writer, gathering
up the Hebrew teaching of many centuries, states quietly and
positively that God has established all things in order once
and for all by the power of His mighty creative Word. Here
is order, not drama and tussle and confusion. It contains the
fullest expression of the writer's theology, his unique witness
to a world lying *outside* God, a reality which exists outside
Himself, though derived from Him and depending upon Him.
Man, he tells us, is made in God's image and likeness. The
whole teaching of the Old Testament develops this theme,
and tells of the struggle between this true conception of a
holy and living God and the mythical and perverted
conceptions of the surrounding cultures, with their jealous,
fighting deities. It is the story of God's love seeking in infinite
patience to find a human vessel through whom He could
make Himself known to His children— children bewildered
and lost in a world full of beauty and terror. Man, made in
God's image, was capable of union with God. This is the
inescapable conviction of the human race, because in this
world man is the highest we know. All true religion is also
convinced, though in different degrees and with different
interpretations of its meaning, that somehow, somewhere,
man has lost or misappropriated this divine capacity, and
hence all the different forms of the story of the Fall. To
this, too, we must attribute the idea of a past, golden age,

and of the perfection of the first man. Yet, as Bishop Gore pointed out in his Bampton lectures many years ago, we have actually no reason for thinking that man was originally perfect. Both St. Irenaeus and Clement of Alexandria expressly denied this. What the Church teaches is that when man's body was first made the dwelling place of a self-conscious, free personality, man might have developed on the lines of God's intention for him, not indeed without effort and struggle, but without rebellion and under no curse. The whole process of the development of the human faculties lay before him. He was adapted to develop freely, but was as yet, nevertheless, imperfect. In Christ alone we see not only 'perfection', and 'freedom' from all taint of sin, but also the *goal* of human development. In Him we see man perfected in God's image, realizing all the divine idea for man. Therefore we can say in very truth that in him the 'End' has come: the end for which man was created.

In the second and third chapters of Genesis, which contain the 'paradise' story, and which were probably written three or four centuries before Genesis 1, we find all the distinctive features of the myths of Paradise, though they have lost much of the colouring of the original conceptions. In the early form of the story primordial Man is divine, or a semi-divine being; the snake a demon, and Paradise the abode of God Himself. In very early mythical thought primordial man was conceived as the gardener of Paradise, and in Mesopotamia the king was thought of as the living representative of this gardener. These two chapters in Genesis actually raise far more questions than they answer, for we must always remember that, in spite of his spiritual and literary genius, the writer himself stood 'outside' Paradise, and not within it. There are many possible interpretations of these two chapters, and this fact makes them all the more fascinating, for it opens up so many questions.

In Genesis 2 we are told that man was created outside Paradise, outside the garden, but that he was brought into the beautiful garden by God in order that he might care for it while living under the divine protection. (vv. 7, 8). This is not the mythical 'garden of God' but a 'garden for man'. We have seen that in many archaic cultures and mythical concepts Paradise is a place where there is no work to be done, everything is provided.   Here in the Yahwist's account there is a sober realism.   In verse 5 he tells us that 'there was not a man to till the ground', so we may draw the obvious conclusion that when man was formed and placed in the garden it was in order that he might till the soil and care for the lovely place in which it had pleased God, in His loving providence, to place him.   The result of the Fall and the curse of which we read later on, lay not in the fact that man would have to work, for work is good and necessary here in this world, but that the result of his labours would be crowned with little success, the land would bring forth 'thorns and thistles'.   In common with the myths, however, he still speaks of the garden as the place where man walked with God.   In this account of Paradise there is little insistence on 'abstruse wonderfulness' (von Rad), and it has really very little in common with the mythical viewpoint.   It is much more 'modern' than the account in Ezekiel which we have considered, and where the mythical colouring is so clearly apparent. The Yahwist shows far more penetration into souls, and his simplicity sets him far apart from the archaic conceptions, though many strands of ancient myth are incorporated into his story.   We must seek to free ourselves from the mythological thinking which has crept into our thoughts on this subject, and approach the account in Genesis with unbiassed eyes.

Obviously many strands of tradition have here been woven together.   In the first place, nowhere else in the Bible do we find the two names for God— Yahweh and Elohim— used interchangeably except in these two chapters.   This may be due to liturgical influence, but it is more likely that it indicates the many strands of myth and tradition gathered together by the writer and interwoven.   According to one tradition Eden was 'Paradise', according to another a 'garden'.   There are also the two diametrically opposed views of sexual relationships which we can discern in these chapters.   The writer is evidently dealing with the two different concepts of the myths of creation and those of Paradise. In the former the union of the sexes is something good, which came into being with the first appearance of woman. In Genesis 2 man obviously rejoiced when he found that he had a true companion and helpmeet: here was equality and possiblity of mutual exchanges and personal relationships. 'Therefore...shall he cleave to his wife: and they shall be one flesh' (2: 24). Here the 'sexual' relationship is clearly taken for granted in Paradise, before the eating of the Tree of Knowledge. Here, too, we see man possessing a certain power of discernment, for though he named the animals he also knew they were not his equals, and could not be his true companions. In chapter 3, however, this discernment appears to follow only after the eating of the Tree of Knowledge, though even here, in v.6, Eve shows some power of discernment and reflection. It has been suggested (Humbert) that between 2:22 and 2:23 there was originally a 'creation myth' which has been expurgated in accordance with Hebrew views regarding matters of sex. The name given in 2:23 'woman' applies to her creation, while that given to her by Adam in 3:20 refers to her function of procreation. In the creation myths the two would have been brought together, but the Yahwist transfers the name 'Eve',— the 'mother of all living'— to the time after the Fall, probably wishing to show that in 'Paradise' there was perfect 'innocence'. Here we see the influence of the 'paradise' myths, which disparage all sexual relations, and in accordance with this view even that 'nakedness' which before the Fall was a symbol of innocence, becomes something obscene after it.

The 'Tree of Knowledge' which is found in Genesis is peculiar to these two chapters, and is not found anywhere else in the Old Testament, on which these chapters have, in fact, made practically no impression: they are conspicuously isolated. No prophet, or psalmist, makes any recognisable reference to the story of the Fall (von Rad) [3]. Here we see the Yahwist in isolation, since he founded neither a tradition nor a school of thought. Though we see hints of other myths

[3] Actually, some commentators have taken Hosea 6-7 to refer to the Genesis story of the Fall.

in his writings his only real source was the revelation he received from God, in the light of which he wrote his account of Paradise.   Therefore, though there is no actual reference to his story in the rest of the Old Testament there are really many links between him and the other writers: the links formed by their common faith.   His work does lie, hiddenly, behind the teaching of the later writers.   In this primeval history all the themes of eschatology and apocalyptic are considered: Paradise, primeval man, peace among the animals, abundance of water etc., and this cannot have found a place here at the beginning of the Hebrew writings without a definite purpose.

CHAPTER VII

THE TREE OF LIFE

THE 'COSMIC TREE' is one of the most ancient of all symbols.
Through the ages it has gathered up into itself various
meanings and associations. The great function of symbols
is, as Paul Tillich has pointed out,

> to point beyond themselves, in the power of that to which
> they point, to open up levels of reality which otherwise are
> closed, and to open up levels of the human mind of which we
> are otherwise unaware. [1]

The symbol reveals something more profound and basic
than objective reality. In the words of Yeats it is 'the only
possible expression of some invisible essence, a transparent
lamp about a spiritual flame'. [2]

The origin of the idea of the cosmic tree is hidden in the
mists of antiquity; it is probably impossible to trace the
place where it first began, and therefore we cannot tell
what its real primary significance was. This symbol is very
widespread, in Eastern and Western cultures, and all the
different meanings attached to this cosmic tree must, as
far as possible, be taken into account. It is, in the first place,
a natural symbol, it shows us the world as a living totality,
regenerating itself periodically, and thus continually fruitful,
with a rich and inexhaustible fruitfulness. It is 'an immediate
intuition of the cipher of the world'. [3] In a sense, the world
speaks through the symbol of the cosmic tree, and its meaning

---

[1] P. Tillich in *Religious Symbolism*.
[2] Quoted by John Wain in *Essays on Literature and Ideas*, p. 121. (Macmillan, 1963).
[3] M. Eliade (ed) in *History of Religions*, p. 98.

is easily understood. The tree is something *living*: year by year it breaks forth into leaf and flower, and possibly fruit; its leaves and flowers fade and die, and at last it stands stripped and bare throughout the winter months. Now this is the fate of all living things, of all that we know as 'life'. Again the tree sends its roots deep down into the earth, its trunk and branches soar up to heaven, and therefore it symbolizes perfectly that three-dimensional concept of the ancients— a concept of immemorial antiquity— of the three levels of earth, heaven and hell. This concept may seem to us childish, and yet there is no other that can express so clearly man's idea of that which is above— God Himself, in whom is all holiness and purity and peace— and the thought that there are depths of evil, all that man instinctively abhors, and which we designate as hell. The ancients thought of the great 'tehôm', the waters on which the earth was thought to float, as the abode of all forms of evil, of monsters, such as the Tiamat of ancient mythology and the 'dragon that is in the sea' of Isaiah (27:1). We cannot take the figure literally, but that to which it points— the three dimensions— are part of the greatest of all mysteries: the ideas of good and evil, of height and depth in the spiritual world. This is something of which even those who have no definite religious faith cannot but be aware, since it is part and parcel of all human thought and experience. The mystery of 'conscience'— the *moral* conscience— of our race has for many theologians been a convincing proof of a righteous and holy God.

There are innumerable variants of this symbol of the cosmic tree, though possibly most of them came from a few centres of diffusion, or even possibly from one such centre. It is not really of value for our special study to trace the history of the symbolism of the 'tree', for what we are seeking to find is its essential meaning: what it reveals and what is shows us in the spiritual history of the human race. Every variant of the symbol emphasizes with particular clarity and intensity some special aspect, and all, as far as possible, must be taken into account. As we have already seen, the 'tree' is a type of the world itself, an *imago mundi* and it is also the 'axis' which on the one hand supports the sky—heaven—and on the other hand reaches down to the deep—hell. It is therefore a 'centre' by which communication is made possible between the three cosmic zones. In other cultures the emphasis is on the tree as a symbol of the periodic regeneration of the world, and its creative possibilities. [4] Therefore, when a tree becomes the object of a cult it is not venerated *as a tree*, but because it is a manifestation of the divine, of the sacred: it refers to supernatural values and points up to God. Since 'inexhaustible life' is the equivalent of immortality it is possible to see in the 'cosmic tree' a symbol of 'life undying'. In primitive thought *inexhaustible life* expressed the idea of *absolute reality*, and hence the tree became the symbol of that reality: the centre of the world.

There are other aspects of this tree symbolism. For the ancients the tree was an expression of *power*. Trees, by their shape and substance, impressed the primitive consciousness. The connection between nature and symbolism reveals to us that intuition of the 'sacred' which was so mysteriously present in the very earliest stages of human life, when man was first able to give expression to his sense of wonder. Because the tree seemed to express something mysterious, something beyond itself, it became a religious object. By its natural laws of development, by 'being there', the tree expressed the primitive conception of the cosmos. Later the tree became a *symbol* of the universe, but at first the tree *was* the universe, just as in the earliest Egyptian thought the king was not only the representative of God, he *was* God. In Babylonian tradition the tree became the dwelling-place of a divinity. In an ancient incantation which has been preserved the tree 'kiškanū' is at 'Eridu', which is the centre of the world. [5] It is thus in a sacred place and at the centre of reality. It is,

---

[4] It is because the Cosmic Tree symbolizes the mystery of the world in perpetual regeneration that it can symbolize, at the same time, and successively, the pillar of the world and the cradle of the human race, the cosmic renovation and the lunar rhythms, the centre of the world, and the path by which we can pass from earth to heaven...Each of these valorizations is possible because from the beginning the symbol of the Cosmic Tree reveals itself as a cypher of the world grasped as a living reality, sacred and inexhaustible.' (M. Eliade, *op. cit.*, p. 94)
[5] M. Eliade, *Patterns in Comparative Religion*, p. 271.

in true mythical terms, of 'shining lapis lazuli', which includes the most perfect of all symbols, that of the 'starry night'. This tree spreads towards the ocean which was thought to surround the world and on which the world floated. It is the true 'sacred tree' which so often appears in the thought of the ancient East. Early Indian tradition represents the cosmos as an *inverted* tree, its roots buried in the sky, its branches spread over the whole earth. This idea may possibly have been suggested by the downpouring rays of the sun. In the *Bhagavad-Gita* the tree expresses not only the universe, but also the condition of man in that universe. It speaks of an indestructible tree, whose roots are above, and whose branches are below: it is the eternal source of life for all beings. Tradition has it that Plato spoke of man as a plant turned upside down, with his roots stretching up to heaven and his branches to the earth. The same tradition of an inverted tree is found in Finnish and Icelandic folklore, and in the Yggdrasil, the ash-tree that in Scandinavian mythology overshadows the world. In Islamic thought the 'tree of happiness' has its roots in heaven and its branches spread over the world.

In Africa and India sap-filled trees are symbols of divine motherhood. In ancient thought Attis is represented by a fir-tree, Osiris by a cedar. In Scandinavian pre-historic monuments it is possible to identify the sacred tree as an oak, and oak leaves are used in their religious art. Apparently one of the reasons for singling out the oak as the 'sacred tree' was that it was the one most frequently struck by lightning— the Fire from Heaven— and this rendered it sacred. According to Frazer the ancient peoples of Europe paid reverence to the oak because they traced a connection between it and the sky-god as it was so frequently struck by lightning. This peculiarity of the oak has actually been established by scientific investigations. In their simple way the ancients may have supposed that the sky-god they worshipped and whose voice they heard in the thunder loved the oak above all the other

---

⁶ Ibid., p. 173.

trees in the wood and therefore descended into it in the lightning flash. A spot where an oak had been struck by lightning was enclosed as a sacred place by the Greeks and Romans. [7] The Mishnah (Sanhedrin 70.a.) declares that the Tree of Knowledge in Genesis was a vine, while the Book of Enoch places the vine between seven mountains. Till quite late grapes and wine went on symbolizing Wisdom. In Mandaism the god of light and wisdom, the redeemer, was also identified with the vine, which was regarded as the cosmic tree because it spread its branches over the heavens. Its grapes were thought to be the stars. The archetypal vine has water within it, its leaves are 'spirits of light', and its nodes fragments of light. The vine, in the vegetable world, expressed immortality, while wine was the symbol of youth and life everlasting.

Now we must consider the two trees which are mentioned in the Genesis account of Paradise, turning our attention first to those explanations which are most in accordance with the thought of the surrounding cultures and with the myths on which much of the description is clearly based, since these were the means by which in those days religious truths were most easily conveyed.

> And the Lord God planted a garden eastward in Eden; and there he put the man whom he had formed. And out of the ground made the Lord God to grow every tree that was pleasant to the sight, and good for food: the tree of life also in the midst of the garden, and the tree of the knowledge of good and evil. (Gen. 2:8-9)

In the Babylonian tradition two identical trees stood at the eastern approach to Heaven: the tree of truth and the tree of life. From the Ras Shamra texts it is possible to gather that Wisdom and Eternity were conferred on man at the same time. Here, quite possibly, is the background of the two trees in Genesis, but what was the actual connection between them? Though the two trees are mentioned in this

---

[7] J. G. Frazer, *The Golden Bough*, (Abridged edition) p. 708.

verse we do not again find any mention of the tree of life
till the end of the third chapter; the tree of the knowledge of
good and evil is alone mentioned. In 2:17 nothing is said
about a tree of life. Did the Yahwist only mention one tree in
the original text, and was the tree of life a later insertion?
Certain scholars think that this is the case, but then it involves
the theory that 3:22, which only mentions the tree of life,
is also a later gloss, and was not in the original text. Again,
are the two trees here mentioned incompatible? Could they
be different aspects of one and the same tree?

In spite of the absence of any further mention of the tree of
life in the Paradise story I think we must, on the basis of the
Babylonian tradition, hold that the two trees were mentioned
in 2:9 in the original account, for there is another possible
explanation which also derives, basically, from the current
myths of the time, but which the wonderfully lucid and
sober account of the Yahwist writer uses to convey a deep
spiritual truth. It is perfectly possible to conclude that
the tree of life was really somewhere in the midst of the
garden, but that its presence there was hidden, just as we
have seen that the precious plant which could bestow perpetual
youth in the Epic of Gilgamesh was hidden at the bottom of
the sea, so that the very knowledge of its existence was only
revealed to Gilgamesh by Utnapishtim, who dwelt with the
gods, and was wise, knowing mysteries. In the Adapa myth,
too, the bread and water of life which could bestow immortality
were only offered to the hero in the heaven of Anu: they
were hidden from mortal eyes. Again, the tree of life in other
cultural traditions was often guarded by a monster, as were
the golden apples in the garden of the Hesperides. The whole
pattern of primeval man seeking everlasting life: the tree of
life, the serpent or monster guarding it, all imply that
immortality is contained in a tree of life (or in a fountain of
life) which is in some inaccessible spot. When man, after
great efforts, approaches the life-giving tree he finds it guarded
by a monster whom he must vanquish in order to attain to that
immortality for which he longs and which he has so ardently
sought. We may think of the long and difficult journey through

the twelve leagues of darkness by which Gilgamesh at last came out into the garden of Paradise which lay by the sea. All this shows clearly that immortality is hard of attainment.

It is also possible that the tree of life in the garden of Paradise was hidden from sight, and that the present place given to it in Genesis 2:9 'in the midst of the garden' was a later interpolation (Humbert). There are many strands of myth and tradition woven into this account, and we must remember that the tree of life was usually placed in the 'garden of God', whereas the Yahwist writer is telling us about a *garden for man*, and there the tree of knowledge comes first into the picture and appears to take the more important place because only by eating of that tree can man come to know of the very existence of a tree of life. Though it is there in the garden all the time man has as yet no inkling of its presence. Only when he has eaten of the tree of the knowledge of good and evil will his eyes be opened to perceive the tree of life. Man was never forbidden to eat of the *tree of life*— that was always something right and laudable— but it was also something hard of attainment. Some scholars, indeed, hold that in the garden of Eden man may have eaten of the tree of life without being aware of its significance, and that he therefore actually enjoyed eternal life without knowing it. [8]

God, in His Wisdom, may possibly have forbidden man to eat of the tree of knowledge because he was not as yet ready for all that it would imply and all that it would demand of him. He sought prematurely for that to which he could not as yet attain.

> Of the tree of the knowledge of good and evil, thou shalt not eat of it: for in the day that thou eatest thereof thou shalt surely die.

Actually, in the event, Adam and Eve do not die after eating of the forbidden fruit, that is, not immediately, though

---

[8] 'Man was created mortal, though if he had continued innocent, he might have secured immortality by eating of the Tree of Life. But immortality, or at least, immortality to be so attained, is out of the question for a sinful being.' Driver, *Genesis*, p. 50.

eventually mankind was thereby deprived of that 'eternal life' which he may have enjoyed, unwittingly, in the garden.

One of the most interesting suggestions on this difficult question is made by Gressmann and Humbert, who hold that the tree of life was actually in the garden of Eden, as Scripture says, but that it was *hidden* from man until he had attained to *knowledge*, that knowledge which alone made it possible for him to discern the tree of life, that is, he was then able to see what the characteristics of that tree were. Till then it had looked to him just like all the other trees in the garden. This we may take to mean that man could have no conception whatsoever of what that 'eternal life' which is signified by the tree of life was, until he had eaten of the fruit of the tree of knowledge: it was something completely outside his horizon— just as it is still outside the thought of the animal creation.

> And the Lord God said, Behold, the man is become as one of us, to know good and evil: and now, lest he put forth his hand, and take also of the tree of life, and eat, and live for ever: therefore the Lord God sent him forth from the garden of Eden (Gen. 3:22-23).

Only after the acquisition of knowledge could the tree of life be discerned. Having eaten of the tree of knowledge man's eyes were opened to see where the tree of life lay, and that meant that henceforth God must guard that precious and lifegiving tree, for this was holy ground, and the holy must be kept sacrosanct:

> So he drove out the man; and he placed at the east of the garden of Eden Cherubims and a flaming sword which turned every way, to keep the way of the tree of life (Gen. 3:24).

We find the tree of life figuring in Chinese and Roman legends, as well as those of Iran. It is the prototype of all miraculous plants. In Christian thought and folklore the Cross of Christ became the 'Tree of Life' *par excellence*. It was said that the wood of the true Cross had power to restore the dead to life, so Helena, the mother of the Emperor

Constantine, went to seek for it in the Holy Land, where she eventually found it. The wood had this power not only because it was that wood upon which Christ died, but because, according to the legend, the Cross was made of the wood of that Tree of Life which had stood in the garden of Eden. The Cross is often depicted in Christian art as the Tree of Life whose roots are in hell and whose summit is the throne of God, while its branches embrace the whole earth. This is beautifully portrayed in a window in Chartres cathedral. It is thus shown as the true 'Centre of the world', that point at which there is communication between the three planes of earth, heaven and hell. In many legends the Cross is also the bridge, or ladder, by which men's souls rise up to God, and it is therefore a thoroughfare between earth and heaven.

One of the most popular legends about Adam and the Tree of Life which was widely current in the Middle Ages said that after Adam had lived in the Hebron valley for 932 years he became fatally ill. In order to find the angel who guarded the gate of Paradise his son, Seth, retraced the steps by which Adam and Eve had left the garden, in which the grass had never grown. On finding the Archangel at the gate of Paradise Seth asked him for some oil of mercy. Hearing his request the Archangel told him to peep into Paradise three times. The first peep showed him the waters of Paradise which were the source of all rivers, with a dried-up tree above them; the second showed him a serpent coiled up at the foot of that tree, while the third time he saw a tree rising up to heaven, its roots spread over the underworld and at its top a newborn child. Since the Tree of Life stood at the centre of the universe it passed through the *axis mundi* and connected the three cosmic spheres. The angel then told Seth that this meant that the Redeemer would come, and gave him three seeds of the tree of which his parents had eaten, and told him to place them on Adam's tongue. Adam, he declared, would die in three days. When Adam was told all this he laughed for the first time since his banishment from Paradise, for he realized that the human race would, after all, be saved. The three seeds placed on his tongue rose up after

his death in the valley of Hebron— three trees growing in
a single span. Seth, knowing their divine origin, transplanted
them to Mount Tabor— the 'centre of the world'— where they
remained for a thousand years till David was told by God
to take them to Jerusalem, which was then also a 'centre'.
Eventually the three trees became one tree, and of this tree the
Cross of Christ was fashioned. The blood of Christ, falling
on the very spot where Adam was born and buried, fell upon
his skull, and thus Adam was redeemed from his sin, and
baptised in the precious blood of Christ. It is a strange story,
but it does serve to show how persistent was the motif of the
life-giving tree, which is set at the 'centre of the world'. [9]

---

[9] A detailed study of this legend and its history may be found in *The Quest of
Seth*, by E. C. Quinn, University of Chicago Press, 1962.

CHAPTER VIII

THE WATERS OF PARADISE

WATER HAS A very wide significance in much religious thought. Its aspects are so varied that here we must leave many of them on one side and concentrate on those which are connected with our theme, though even here we shall be able only to deal very briefly with a subject which is so rich in its symbolism.

The lands of the Near East, where water is often very scarce, are dependent on water for their very existence. A drought in Spring may well spell ruin and famine for many. In Babylonia, Egypt, and Palestine water was therefore associated with life-giving properties, and in Egyptian belief especially the divine waters could give life in every conceivable form. Water issuing from the earth was regarded as coming from the womb of the earth-mother, and to be plunged into these waters was to gain immortality. A descent into water symbolized a new penetration into mysterious depths from which true creativity could be derived. There were very vague notions in the entire ancient world about the origin and the course of the great rivers. So great did the Nile appear to them that its source might have been at any distance. Alexander the Great, for instance, took the Indus for the upper course of the Nile. Thus it is not surprising that the garden of Eden was thought to be the source of all the great rivers in the world. The great mother-stream, which watered all the known world, was so great and so precious that it must be part of the 'paradisal' creation. In this connection it is interesting to consider the passage in Genesis which speaks of the great rivers which take their rise in Eden.

Most scholars now consider that the passage describing the four rivers in Genesis 2:10-14 is an interpolation into the original text. We will briefly enumerate their reasons for this con-

clusion.   In the first place, these four verses conflict with the
location of Paradise in Genesis 2:8 and 3:24, where it is said
to lie to the east of Canaan.   Here, on the other hand, Paradise
is located as the source of the great rivers Tigris and Euphrates,
that is, among the Armenian mountains north of Palestine.
Furthermore, this passage interrupts the flow of the narrative,
which shows it to be a later gloss, an insertion of a 'paradise'
myth into the Yahwist's account.   Again the somewhat fanciful
description is more in keeping with the mythical thought of the
surrounding cultures than with the sobriety and simplicity of
the Yahwist's narrative.   Surely, too, had the latter written this
passage he would have said 'a river which the Lord God made
to go out of Eden to water the garden', or something on those
lines, instead of simply stating 'a river went out of Eden to
water the garden' without any mention of the divine creator.

Whoever wrote this passage was content with nothing less
than a map of the whole world, or at least, the world that was
then known.   He tells us of the wonderful stream, whose source
was unknown, but the magic power of which was so great that
it could only originate in Paradise itself, wherever that might
be.   This river, having watered the garden of Eden, issued out of
it as one great stream, but was then parted into four main rivers:

> A river went out of Eden to water the garden: and from
> thence it parted, and became into four heads (Gen. 2: 10).

The first of these encompasses 'the whole land of Havilah'
which was the country inhabited by the descendants of Havilah,
the son of Cush.   This river is difficult to identify, but the
description of the land it encompasses has some echoes of the
'wonderfulness' of the ancient myths:

> the gold of that land is good: there is bdellium and the
> onyx stone (2:11).

The ancients divided the Nile into two— the upper and the
lower Nile— and it is possible that the first river was one part
of it.   The second river is probably the Nubian Nile, the third
Tigris and the fourth Euphrates.   What a tremendous amount

of water there must have been in Eden if the river, having watered the garden, could still enclose the entire world in its four arms, and fructify it. All the waters outside Paradise, which supply all the civilizations, are, so to speak, only a remainder or residue of the waters of Paradise. This passage in Genesis undoubtedly seeks to sketch the real geographical world. There is a close connection here between earth and the garden on the one hand, and the historical world of men on the other. The object is, apparently, to emphasize the topical significance of Eden, or the garden of Paradise, for man outside Paradise, by showing the unbroken stream of water flowing from Paradise and bringing life to the whole earth. This may account for the insertion here of the 'mythical' passage, which would give it a very profound significance. The four streams of Genesis 2 testify to the goodness of God who wishes to fertilize the whole earth and thus to make the whole world habitable. This thought may also be applied to Genesis 2:6, where fertility has its beginning. We shall see later on how this thought was developed by the Prophets in their writings.

In the Old Testament there are frequent references to the vivifying power of water, and the dire consequences of its absence. Isaiah's threat to the sinners in Jerusalem who abandon Yahweh is

Ye shall be as a garden that hath no water (Is. 1:30).

In another place he speaks of the chiefs of Israel as being like 'rivers of water in a dry place' (32:2).

The Deutero-Isaiah compares the effects of water with the outpouring of the spirit of God: the spirit is thought of primarily as the power of life which springs up and develops irresistibly wheresoever it manifests itself:

I will pour water upon him that is thirsty, and floods upon the dry ground:
I will pour my spirit upon thy seed, and my blessing upon thine offspring:
And they shall spring up as among the grass, as willows by the water courses (Is. 44:3-4).

In Jeremiah men and trees are brought together and compared. Water is that which gives life to the trees, but that
which gives life to men is not named, so clearly the missing term
can only be God, who is thus likened to water. The miraculous
effect of water is the starting-point for the miracle of faith:

> Blessed is the man that trusteth in the Lord, and whose hope
> the Lord is. For he shall be as a tree planted by the waters,
> and that spreadeth out her roots by the river, and shall not
> see when heat cometh, but her leaf shall be green: and shall
> not be careful in the year of drought, neither shall cease from
> yielding fruit (Jer. 17:7-8).

What water does for nature, that God himself does for the
faithful. Water gives life and enables the trees to bring forth
fruit. Trees planted by the waterside need not fear times of
drought, for their leaf remains green and they are still able to
bear fruit. In like manner God will enable his children to bear
fruit in spite of trials, and their life will continue despite their
present sufferings. When Israel is restored 'their soul shall be
as a watered garden; and they shall not sorrow any more at
all' (Jer. 31:12). Again, using the same simile, Jeremiah
speaks neither of trees or of men, but of the soul of the believer,
which is like a watered garden:

> I have satiated the weary soul, and I have replenished every
> sorrowful soul (31: 25).

Jeremiah is the prophet of the inner life of union with God—
that interior life which alone sustained Adam in the Garden
of Eden when the race of man had as yet no other means of
knowing God. The loss of this interior life of simple union with
God— a union which, nevertheless, was probably unrealized for
what it was, but was taken for granted, just as a child lives in
simple confidence in the love of its parents without considering
what it means— was in great measure lost at the Fall. In the
sufferings of the Exile, when all the things which distract men
and turn their eyes to outward things were torn away from them,
some of the Israelites were able once more to find God speaking

to their hearts. Jeremiah's record of familiar intercourse with God is very precious, throwing a new light on the way of God and the way of man. In the light of his inner union with God he looked about him and saw the true meaning of sin, its essential roots. God had given him much, and he realized with the vividness which only comes to the mystic the wonder of God's love, and of His yearning longing for a response to that love. Israel's forgetfulness of God's love seemed to him to be the very essence of sin. This recognition of the *inwardness* of sin was the great contribution made by Jeremiah to the truth about man. He saw that sin was stubbornness of heart.

In the Old Testament generally water is essentially a vivifying and fertilizing element, and a *moving* one. Water coming from above signifies wisdom, and in the Wisdom literature water and wisdom are compared. On account of its transparency water is also a symbol of innocence:

> I will wash my hands in innocency; so will I go to thine altar, O Lord (Ps. 26:6).

God's power over nature in all its forms is one of the leading ideas of the Bible. Since the ocean was always in a sense terrifying, unaccountable, God's supreme power was especially manifested in His power over the sea, either in stirring up the waves or in giving calm: a point brought out very strikingly in the beautiful little book of Jonah. In piling up the waters of the Red Sea so that the children of Israel might go over dryshod, and in drowning their pursuers, God's power shone forth so clearly that we find this incident compared with the original creation. Again in the crossing of Jordan by Joshua the same power was manifested. Whether this was a natural event which happened to take place at the right moment, or a 'miracle', is really of little importance, for in both cases the hand of God was there, behind it, and His saving power shone forth through that outward event with a transparent clarity, producing faith.

In Babylonian thought, too, floods and drought were caused by a god. We find Adad described as 'Master and Lord' of the sources of the rain, of the flood, and of the Deluge.

It is he who gives the storm and the great tempests, but they are of little account in comparison with the great Flood, in which God's power over the cosmos was most plainly manifested.   Not only the rains obey him, but also the source of the rains, which at his command poured out the waters that caused the Flood.   In ancient times earth was thought to float on the waters of the great abyss, while above were the waters of heaven in which windows were opened to let down the rain.   It was uncertain whether the Flood was caused by the uprising of the deep or the downpouring of rain from heaven: possibly it was a mixing of the two, the salt waters and the sweet which should not be mixed.

The important point to notice, however, is the difference between the attitude of Yahweh and that of the Babylonian deities, such as we find in the ancient epics.   The God of the Bible, at the moment when the catastrophe begins, holds Himself in some way *above* the event, He is transcendent, and not involved in the Flood Himself.   In the same way He is always shown to be in command of every situation, always in perfect control:

> The Lord sitteth upon the flood: yea, the Lord sitteth King for ever (Ps. 29: 10).

In such epics as that of Gilgamesh, on the other hand, the deities are overwhelmed and can only flee, fear and lament, blaming one another for the catastrophe:

> Even the gods were terrified at the flood, and they fled to the highest heaven, the firmament of Anu; they crouched against the walls, cowering like curs.   Then Ishtar, the sweet-voiced Queen of Heaven cried out like a woman in travail: "Alas, the days of old are turned to dust because I commanded evil; why did I command this evil in the council of the gods?   I commanded wars to destroy the people, but are they not my people, for I brought them forth?   Now like the spawn of fish they float on the ocean."   The great gods of heaven and of hell wept, they covered their mouth. [1]

[1] *The Epic of Gilgamesh*, pp. 107, 8.

There is no assurance anywhere; no strong power on which the people in their need can rely. This pessimism and bewilderment come out strongly in this Epic, and give to it a strange pathos.

In Genesis, however, the God in whom his people trust promises that this destructive act will not be repeated (9:11); there will not be another cataclysm, but instead of it a work of redemption. Thus in the Old Testament we usually find that the waters of the earth which are dominated by the almighty God are a source of blessing. He 'laid the foundations of the earth that it should not be removed for ever'; He covered it with the deep 'as with a garment', the 'waters stood above the mountains:

> At thy rebuke they fled; at the voice of thy thunder they hasted away. They go up by the mountains; they go down by the valleys unto the place which thou hast founded for them. Thou hast set a bound that they may not pass over; that they turn not again to cover the earth. (Ps. 104:7-9)

God sends the springs into the valleys 'which run among the hills. They give drink to every beast of the field; the wild asses quench their thirst.'

> He watereth the hills from his chambers: the earth is satisfied with the fruit of thy works.
> He causeth the grass to grow for the cattle, and herb for the service of men: that he may bring forth food out of the earth: and wine that maketh glad the heart of man, and oil to make his face shine, and bread which strengtheneth man's heart. The trees of the Lord are full of sap... He appointed the moon for seasons; the sun knoweth his going down (Ps. 104: 13-15, 19).

Having enumerated all his works and the great mercies of his God the psalmist cries out in wonder

> O Lord, how manifold are thy works! In wisdom hast thou made them all; the earth is full of thy riches, so is the great and wide sea also, wherein are things creeping innumerable,

both small and great beasts. There go the ships; there is
that leviathan whom thou hast made to play therein. These
wait all upon thee: that thou mayest give them their meat in
due season. That thou givest them they gather, thou openest
thine hand and they are filled with good (Ps. 104:24-28).

How different is the atmosphere breathed in these lovely
lines. Whereas the other cultures saw in the water simply a
great cosmic power, the Israelites felt that water and all nature
was ordained by God for their good, to bring life and joy. The
climate of Palestine rendered water an absolute necessity, as
drought could so easily lead to famine: an east wind blowing
in March or April could dry up everything very quickly if
there was not sufficient rain, and therefore rain was regarded
as a special blessing and a gift of God. The psalmist speaks of
'a dry and thirsty land where no water is' (63:1), but is also
convinced that 'the river of God is full of water':

Thou visitest the earth and waterest it: thou greatly enrichest
it with the river of God, which is full of water: thou preparest
them corn, when thou hast so provided for it. Thou waterest
the ridges thereof abundantly... thou makest it soft with
showers: thou blessest the springs thereof (Ps. 65:9,10).

In primitive thought streams and torrents were often believed
to be under the influence of local 'numen' or spirits, but in
the Old Testament, (except perhaps in a few of the earliest
contexts) they all come under the power of Yahweh. In psalm
98:8 however, we find the psalmist crying

Let the floods clap their hands: let the hills be joyful together,
before the Lord.

There is a kind of personification of nature. Ezekiel, too,
is told to prophesy against mountains and rivers:

Ye mountains of Israel, hear the word of the Lord God: Thus
saith the Lord God to the mountains, and to the hills, to the
rivers and to the valleys: Behold I, even I, will bring a sword
upon you (6:3).

This is characteristic of very primitive thinking. In some texts, too, there is a ' mythical ' reference to the Nile, and Pharaoh represents the primordial enemy. The fight between him and Yahweh is conceived very much on the lines of that between Tiamat and Marduk in the *Enuma Elish* which was read at the Babylonian New Year Festival. God's enmity with Pharaoh is really with the Nile, which Pharaoh claimed to have created. God must show that He alone was the creator of the Nile and none other:

> Thus saith the Lord God: Behold, I am against thee, Pharaoh, King of Egypt, the great dragon that lieth in the midst of his rivers, which hath said, My river is mine own, and I have made it for myself (Ezek. 29:3).

And again:

> The land of Egypt shall be desolate and waste: and they shall know that I am the Lord: because he hath said, The river is mine and I have made it (29:9).

It is difficult to tell which myths have really influenced these texts in the Old Testament. God shows His power by calming the Nile so that it flows like oil, bringing peace and calm. In the New Testament, likewise, Jesus quells the storm that rises so suddenly as his disciples are crossing the sea, and they are filled with amazement, saying 'Who is this that even the sea and the winds obey him?' (St. Mark 4:41).

In Indian thought water is the source of all things. In a text which sums up a long Vedic tradition we find the words:

> Water, thou art the source of life and of all existence [2]

Waters are conceived as the foundation of the whole world, they precede and uphold all creation and every cosmic manifestation. Therefore, since water is the source of all things, we can see why there are myths and legends which make it the

---

[2] *Bhavisyottarapurana*, 31, 14.

origin of the human race, or at least of some parts of it. The
Karaja Indians of Brazil still claim to be able to recall the time
when they 'lived in the water', and there is a 'children's sea'
on the south coast of Java. [3] Immersion in water implies a
return to the preformal condition; a regeneration, a new birth,
for it means a dissolution of forms, a return to the original state.
To emerge from the water is, consequently, a repetition of the
act of creation, a re-creation. Every dissolution is followed by
a 'new birth', because immersion fertilizes, and thus increases
the potentialities of life. Because water contains in itself all
potentialities it becomes a symbol of life, and we can thus speak
of 'living water'. The Song of Songs refers to 'A fountain of
gardens, a well of living waters, and streams from Lebanon'.
(4:15), and the Deutero-Isaiah cries

> Ho, everyone that thirsteth, come ye to the waters, and he that
> hath no money, come ye, buy and eat; yea, come, buy wine
> and milk, without money and without price (55:1).

In St. John's Gospel we read that Jesus, speaking to the
Samaritan woman as he sat on Jacob's well, said to her

> If thou knewest the gift of God, and who it is that saith to thee,
> 'Give me to drink'; thou wouldest have asked of him, and he
> would have given thee living water... whosoever drinketh
> of the water that I shall give him shall never thirst; but the
> water that I shall give him shall be in him a well of water
> springing up into everlasting life (Jn. 4:10-14).

This passage fulfils and illuminates two aspects of water in
the thought of the ancient world. A fragment from the second
stratum of the bronze age at Megiddo shows a palm tree which,
in place of the two lower branches on either side, has a stream
flowing to the earth. The palm seems to take the place of a
god. Here then is the tree of life and the water of life which we
find in the paradise story in Genesis. Other archeological
discoveries illustrate the same idea, which was evidently preva-

---

[3] M. Eliade, *Patterns in Comparative Religion*, pp. 188ff.

lent at that period.   It has been noted that in the Old Testament the two are carefully not brought together, probably with
the idea of evading the heathen combination of tree and water.
For example, in Proverbs we find the tree of life mentioned
repeatedly (3:18; 11:30; 13:12; 15:4) and also the water of
life (10:11; 13:14; 14:27; 16:22), but they are very carefully
kept apart in order to avoid the mythical idea that the water
of life flows from a tree or a tree-god.   The true thought of the
Hebrew is expressed by the psalmist in psalm 36: 9:

'For with thee is the fountain of life'.

Thus in the Old Testament the myths of the tree of life and
the water of life flowing from it are broken: Yahweh alone is
the author of life and can be to us both tree and water of life.
When Jesus claims to be able to give the water of life he does so
as the Son of God.   And yet, how richly prophetic, in its own
way, that early concept was!   Secondly, there was a widely
prevalent belief in Egypt, Mesopotamia and Sumeria that the
departed were tortured by thirst.   Therefore they must be
refreshed and water was placed in their graves, or conduits
were made into the tombs by which the living might supply
water to the dead.   The ancients seem to have been much
concerned with this thought of the thirst of the departed, since,
in their belief, only the very best were given water in the beyond.
Though this custom of supplying water for the dead was so
prevalent in the surrounding cultures there is no sign of it
among the Hebrews.   When then Jesus spoke to the Samaritan
woman and told her 'whosoever drinketh of the water that I
shall give him shall never thirst; but the water that I shall give
him shall be in him a well of water springing up into everlasting
life', the 'never' may be seen to apply not only to this present
life but also to the life after death, and thus this concern which
was felt in the heathen world would be assuaged.
    The prototype of all water is 'living water'— water that
comes from some holy place, from the garden of Paradise, or
from the heavens above.   Underlying this very prevalent idea
is the same fundamental thought that *reality* is somehow concen-

trated in a living substance from which all living forms proceed, either directly or by 'symbolic participation '.[4]   Water animals, and especially fish, are therefore sacred symbols because they stand for that absolute reality which is concentrated in water. Again the 'ageless river', the 'living water' flows by the tree of life, the miraculous tree.   In the Revelation of St. John the two symbols are brought together:

> And he shewed me a pure river of water of life, clear as crystal, proceeding out of the throne of God and of the Lamb.   In the midst of the street of it, and on either side of the river, was there the tree of life, which bare twelve manner of fruits, and yielded her fruit every month: and the leaves of the tree were for the healing of the nations (Rev. 22:1-2).

The immemorial symbolism of immersion in water was adopted by Christianity and given a fuller and richer meaning, but all that may be called the 'pre-history' of christian baptism sought the same object, though at different levels.   There can be no question here of outside influence or of borrowing from other cultures, for this is a universal conception: it is 'archetypal'.   The symbolism of water is the result of an intuition of the cosmos as a 'unity', and of man as a 'specific mode of being in the cosmos. [5]

[4] O. Kaiser, *Die Mythische Bedeutung des Meeres*, p. 109.

[5] M. Eliade, *op. cit.*, p. 197.

Dr. Dillistone has also pointed out in his book on *Christianity and Symbolism* that :

'There is ample evidence from psycho-analytical investigations to show that water is the commonest archetypal image of the unconscious, and that a descent into water is normally a symbolic description of a new penetration into those deeper and more mysterious fecundities from which a true creativity can be derived.   Other elements are associated with water in this dim realm of the unconscious— the void, darkness, death, silence, loneliness— but water gathers them all together' (p. 183.).

He shows that water gushing from the earth is regarded as issuing from the womb of the earth-mother, and that to be plunged into this water was to gain the gift of immortality.   To descend into still water was to return to the source of creativity. (p. 185).

These ideas all entered into the teaching of the early Fathers on Baptism, in which there is a possibility 'of touching the deepest level of the "general memory" or the "collective unconscious", and to see Baptism in this way, and realize what it implies is "one of the most urgent tasks of our day".' (p. 187.)

The very fact that water flows, and moves, and springs up from the earth, shows it to be a living substance. Springs and rivers display power, perpetual renewal, and life. We know that they *are*, and that they are alive, and therefore the religious significance of water persists and is found in all religions, in spite of all efforts to suppress it. In whatever religious framework it appears water has the same value: it purifies and gives new life, it washes away sins, and when it is employed in rituals it brings the fleeting moment of time out of ordinary 'profane' time into that great sacred time which was 'in the beginning', the time when the world was created. Living water bestows eternal life and renews youth. Consequently water gradually came to be regarded as powerful for healing and for fertility. All over Europe we find 'holy wells' whose waters are for healing. In India thousands flock to bathe in the holy waters of the Ganges; from all over the world Catholics go to Lourdes to seek healing of body and mind, and for the refreshment of their souls, in that miraculous stream that springs from the Pyrenean hillside. Whether their bodily ills are cured matters less, apparently, than the fact that they come away with holy joy singing in their hearts. We are not far here from that ageold conception of the waters that stream forth from the garden of Paradise to water all the earth.

CHAPTER IX

WHERE ART THOU?

W HAT WAS THE real meaning of the serpent's words to Eve in Genesis 3:5?

> God doth know that in the day ye eat thereof, your eyes shall be opened, and ye shall be as gods, knowing good and evil.

There are many theories, many possible interpretations. It is now probably agreed that no purely moral, ethical sense may be given to these words, to this 'knowledge'. Comparing the Hebrew word used here with other passages in the Old Testament where it occurs it becomes clear that it implies *practical* knowledge, and not something merely theoretical. To give a few examples: in 1 Kings 9:27 it is used of the knowledge 'shipmen' have of the sea, in Esther 1:13a the wise men 'knew the times', while in 13b they also knew the law and judgement. 'Hearken unto me ye that know righteousness' says the Deutero-Isaiah (51:7). In Daniel 11:32 'the people that do know their God shall be strong'. So when the serpent says 'ye shall be as gods, knowing good and evil' experimental knowledge is implied. They will know, they will gain experience. Before the Fall man had no theoretical or experimental knowledge any more than the animal creation has now. The fruit of the 'Tree of Knowledge' will bring a 'general' knowledge, which implies powers of discernment and practical ability. It is not only knowledge, but also experience, or 'wisdom' in the deepest and fullest sense of the word. Pedersen, that great authority on the Israelites, has said:

> The logic of the Israelites was not abstract logic, but an immediate perception. [1]

[1] J. Pedersen, *Israel*, 1926, p. 124.

He showed further that knowledge of something implied *intimacy* with it. To *know* a thing or a person is to be intimate with it. [2]

Eve, pondering the words of the serpent saw that

> the tree was good for food, and that it was pleasant to the eyes, and a tree to be desired to make one wise.

'To make one wise'. This, when compared with the numerous texts in which the Hebrew word for 'wise' occurs in the Old Testament may be taken to imply either the idea of 'instruction', as in psalm 2:10:

> Be wise now, therefore, O ye kings: be instructed, ye judges of the earth.

or in Proverbs 1:3:

> To receive instruction of wisdom, justice, and judgment.

Or it may convey the thought of attention, reflection, comprehension, listening or prudence. Examples of this are to be found in some of the earliest Books of the Bible:

> O that they were wise, that they understood this, that they would consider their latter end (Deut. 32:29).
> Therefore the prudent shall keep silence in that time (Amos 5:13).

The Deutero-Isaiah gives us a very clear example of its use:

> That they may see, and know, and consider, and understand together, that the hand of the Lord hath done this, and the Holy One of Israel hath created it (41: 20).

In some places, it is true, it conveys the sense of success or prosperity, as in Joshua 1:7:

> that thou mayest prosper (or 'do wisely') whithersoever thou goest.

---

[2] Ibid. p. 109.

This meaning, however, must probably be excluded from Genesis 3:6. The other two meanings are actually very closely connected with each other. The first is found more frequently in the later books of the Bible, and in the Wisdom literature, while the second is found in some of the earliest books, in the Law and the Prophets, and is therefore 'pre-exilic'. The idea of 'instruction' cannot be excluded from Genesis 3:6, for the tree can confer instruction 'magically and immediately' and to be instructed and to be wise are closely connected meanings. Man will become instructed and intelligent, wise and powerful, capable and knowledgeable in all ways, in place of the innocence which was his before the 'Fall', that is, before the eating of the fruit of the 'forbidden tree'. [3]

The eyes of them both were opened, and they knew they were naked; and they sewed fig leaves together, and made themselves aprons (Gen. 3: 7).

This sense of 'nakedness' we usually attribute to the disorder introduced by sin and disobedience, or possibly to the realization of 'sex' and the feeling of shame which seems to characterize all matters connected with it in the human mind, and certainly in Hebrew thought. There have, however, been other interpretations which are of interest. The Greek Fathers of the Early Church saw in Adam's feeling of nakedness a very simple reaction to cold, to counteract which he sewed fig leaves together to clothe himself with. They taught that this sense of physical need, of nakedness, was to lead men to make many and great discoveries: 'necessity was the mother of invention'. Man, left to himself, felt the need of covering which was to lead him to exercise his inventive faculties. We see here two ways of approaching this initial catastrophe of the human race: there is the emphasis on it *as* a catastrophe in which man turned away from his original and essential condition, but there is, on the other hand, the thought that man's sense of weakness and cold

[3] P. Humbert, *Études sur le récit de Paradis et de la Chute dans la Genèse* (1940), p. 95.

led him to use his intelligence as he would not otherwise have done.   These two aspects may, however, be brought together if we think, in accordance with St. Basil, that man, turning away from intercourse with God, became wholly occupied with material things and his physical needs which turned his thoughts away from God.   Man could no longer see divine things with the simplicity that was his in the garden of Eden, he ceased to enjoy that intercourse with God which was primarily his only means of knowing divine things, his interior life became blurred by his preoccupation with the things of sense.   St. Basil thought that men did not really need clothing any more than the animal creation, and if they had always remained in Paradise God would have seen to it that they were kept warm and properly fed.   This idea is found in some of the lives of the Desert Fathers related by Palladius, Bishop of Helenopolis, a friend of St. John Chrysostom, in his 'Paradise of the Holy Fathers'.   He records the lives of two monks in the 'inner desert' who went naked and lived with the beasts.   Abbot Macarius, finding them, asked, ' When it is winter are ye not frozen? And in the season of heat are not your bodies consumed? '   Whereupon they made answer, 'God in his providence hath made us to be so that in winter we do not freeze, and in the summer we are not burned up.'   Again, he tells of a certain old man who lived with the buffaloes and subsisted on the fruit of a palm tree which grew by his cave, and which produced twelve clusters of dates each year, yielding him food for each month.   After thirty years spent in this way he declared that the climate always supplied him in moderation with what was necessary. [4] The result of the Fall was that man became excessively preoccupied with the thought of his physical needs, and technical knowledge was to detract from the knowledge of God.   The Cappadocian Fathers taught that man was created neither mortal nor immortal, but capable of either.

While man lived in the Garden of Eden, in Paradise, he was really in a state of 'ecstasy', and was therefore unconscious of any physical needs.   Like the animal creation he was content

[4] *Op. cit.*, p. 62.

to wander in the garden and bask in the sun and eat the berries
and fruit he found to hand. At the Fall all this was changed:
man realized his physical needs. Adam and Eve, realizing
their nakedness, possibly experiencing the feeling of cold, were no
longer able to remain idle, and sewed leaves together in order
to clothe themselves with them and keep out the cold. Origen,
the Alexandrian Platonist of the 3rd century and one of the
greatest and most devoted scholars the Church has ever known,
saw in this sense of need which led to the use of man's innate
and superior faculties something better than that state of abundance which gave no impetus to the exercise of those faculties.
Abundance, he showed, could be a bad thing for man. God
sent his angels to care for man and supply his needs till
man was ready to seek God for himself, till the moment when
he was driven not only to supply his own physical needs but
also to seek God for himself.

Père Teilhard de Chardin, in his great work on 'The Phenomenon of Man', sought to develop a coherent perspective of the
extended experience of man— 'a whole which unfolds'. [5] He
declared that the time had now come when we must seek an
interpretation of the *interior* as well as the *exterior* of things, of
mind as well as of matter. Man in his wholeness must some
day be included in a true picture of the world, and in this
picture man must not be seen as static, but as the leading shoot
of evolution. He showed that there is a double aspect to the
structure of the universe: that 'co-extensive with their *without*
there is also a *within* of things'. This he declared to be the
only possible picture of the world, though the thought may well
daunt our imagination. He showed, further, that this within
really has the same meaning as 'consciousness' and 'spontaneity'. He speaks of a 'determinate' without and 'fire' within— two aspects we find in the cosmos which are neither irre-
ducible nor incommensurable. Everywhere in the universe
there is a conscious *inner* face which duplicates the material
external face which is alone commonly considered by science.
He suggests that we go further and define the rules by which

[5] *Op. cit.*, p. 35.

that usually hidden, inner face suddenly shows itself and bursts through into certain other regions of experience. A richer and better organized structure will always correspond to a more fully developed consciousness: even the simplest form of protoplasm is already a substance of unheard of complexity. Spiritual perfection (or 'centreity') and material synthesis (or complexity) are two aspects or connected parts of one single phenomenon. Here we come to the crux of the matter, and we see the gradual development first of all of the invisibility, then the gradual appearance and then the *dominance* of the within in comparison with the without of things. Père de Chardin sought to develop the story of this struggle in the universe between the unified *multiple* and the unorganized multitude: the 'full application of the great law of *complexity and consciousness*'. He pointed out that undoubtedly there is something through which material and spiritual energy are held together and are complementary. Yet we cannot couple them together, for as soon as we try to do this their mutual independence becomes as clear as their interrelation. They are constantly associated, and pass into each other, but it is impossible to establish a simple correspondence between them. Only a minute fraction of 'physical' energy is used up in the exercise of 'spiritual' energy. The whole universe is constantly being drawn forwards to a greater complexity and centreity. Between this within and without of things the interdependence of energy is, nevertheless, incontestable, though it can only be expressed in complex symbolism. The whole tends to be 'centred', and the more centred it becomes the greater its power. It seems that the whole universe tends to be centred in an 'Omega' point. [6]

After this digression, which may help to clarify our theme, we must return to the verses we are now considering in Genesis. We have seen that in Paradise, or Eden, man lived, apparently, much the same life as the animals, though he was from the first superior to the rest of created beings. The Yahwist writer shows man's relationship to the animal world:

---

[6] Ibid., pp. 56-64.

And out of the ground the Lord formed every beast of the field, and every fowl of the air; and he brought them to Adam to know what he would call them. . . and Adam gave names to all cattle, and to the fowl of the air, and to every beast of the field (Gen. 2:19-20).

Yet none of these were able to be his true companions on account of their inferiority— they lived on a different level— and therefore God created woman out of the rib of Adam's body and she became his helpmeet, his equal. We have also seen that in the archaic cultures of the present day there is still the idea of returning to that time which was *in the beginning*, when all was as it should be, and that one of the means of attaining the ecstasy which, for a short time, brings the mystic, or shaman, into that paradisal state of existence is to enter into a closer relationship with the animal world by imitating its cries and sounds. In some primitive cultures certain animals are regarded as sacred. Now, without considering any further the difference between men and animals we must come to the point which alone bears on our subject. Though, admittedly, the animal *knows*, it *cannot know that it knows*, that is quite certain. It does not possess the power of *reflection*. This is the point where man rises immeasurably above the lower creation. We may be disturbed to find how little we differ from the animals in our physical make-up, in spite of our mental pre-eminence. At some point, apparently, man came to the power of reflection. His mental powers were brought, as it were, to 'boiling point, and some further calories were added' . This was sufficient to disturb man's whole equilibrium, for 'what was primarily only a centred surface, became a centre'. Outwardly almost nothing in man's organs was changed, but in depth a great evolution had taken place:

> consciousness was now leaping and boiling in a space of super-sensory relationships and representations: and simultaneously consciousness was capable of perceiving itself in the concentrated simplicity of its faculties. And all this happened for the first time. [8]

[7] Ibid., p. 165.
[8] Ibid., p. 168.

Père de Chardin pointed out that it was an accepted principle of Christian thought that there were different and succes-
sive planes of knowledge— discontinuity in continuity.   The
consciousness of each one of us as we look at ourselves is evolution looking at itself. [9]   The more man becomes truly man the
more he will seek to move towards that which is new, towards
the 'absolute'.   Evolution gives rise to consciousness, and
consciousness leads to union.   The outcome of the world, the
gates of the future, the entry into the 'super-human' are not for
the privileged few but for all together.   The stuff of the universe,
by becoming *thinking*, has not yet completed its evolutionary
cycle, and we are moving forward to some central point ahead.
What we still lack is a new domain of psychical expansion, and
this, if we would but lift up our heads, is staring us in the face.
Yet, in spite of the attraction that is always at work to bring
mankind together, thinking units do not seem capable at present
of falling into the radius of that attractive, magnetic energy.
Men remain hostile and closed in to each other.   Here, clearly,
is a profound perversion.

We have seen that in Genesis 3:7 we are shown that man
responded to this new urge to thought and to reflection in the
physical sense.   Yet, together with this call to greater external
advance, to scientific thought and to self-development, there
came a call to an equal advance in the life of the spirit, and to
this call man could not at that stage respond.   Man did, in
fact, respond to the new vision that came to him by making
more and more use of those hidden treasures which were there
in the physical universe, ready to be used, but awaiting the
moment, or moments, when man should discover them.   God,
who created all things by the power of his mighty Word, knows
and has known from all eternity all those secrets which we in
this twentieth century are discovering in the material universe
to our great joy and satisfaction.   Man has found many ways
of clothing and feeding himself which earlier generations would
scarcely have believed possible.   And on this point Origen was
surely right.   Had man always remained in the primal Paradise,

[9] Ibid., p. 221.

cared for and protected by the angels of God, how much less varied and delightful our world would have been, and after all, the world into which we are born *is* the only world we know and the only world we can conceive, and we must look at it as we find it and say that, in very many ways, it is *very good*. We must therefore set aside the idea that it would have been better if man had not *fallen* into activity and used his faculties to make life more and more complex and beautiful and satisfying. It was not this that constituted the fall of man. It was rather that which follows:

> And they heard the voice of the Lord God walking in the garden in the cool of the day: and Adam and his wife hid themselves from the presence of the Lord God amongst the trees of the garden. And the Lord called unto Adam, and said unto him, Where art thou? And he said, I heard thy voice in the garden, and I was afraid, because I was naked, and I hid myself (Gen. 3:8-10).

Here, according to one Rabbinic text, was the first Shekinah, the first appearance of God's glory in this world. Everything in the paradisal stage of man's existence had been 'very good' as far as it went: God provided for him as he did for the lower creation, for whom He still provides in this way, until the moment came when man was ready to advance to a further stage of progress, and when he had to be encouraged to fend for himself and use his own intelligence so that it might develop ever more and more to the glory of his Creator. Man found himself at some juncture— the turning point in his progress— able to reflect, to think about the world in which he found himself placed. This power of reflection is mirrored in the mythical thought and tradition that have come down through so many centuries, and reach as far back as our records go. [10]

---

[10] At some timeless moment God made the experiment of creating human spirits capable of choice, capable of finding their fullest life in knowing and loving Him, and being known and loved by Him. All the creation myths are but a faint and distorted image of this original truth, and therefore contribute in their measure to the pattern of revelation... Other myths...bear witness to the fact that at some point ... a breach occurred between God and man— man chose to be independent of God, and cut off from the source of his freedom, became a slave (S.H. Hooke, *Alpha and Omega*, p. 5).

In the fertility cults there was the annual repetition of the primeval events by which man thought he might obtain the favour
of the gods and fruitfulness for man and beast. In these early
cults and rites there was also the desire to escape from 'profane'
time and to enter into the 'Sacred Great Time', into which
they actually believed themselves to be able to enter during the
time of the cult ritual. There was also the longing to share in
the life of the gods, in immortality. In these verses, however,
the Yahwist writer— that brilliant unknown spiritual genius—
strikes a note we have not heard before, but which was to ring
through the whole of the Old Testament, and indeed, through
the whole of the New:

The Lord God called unto Adam... and he hid himself.

The account of Paradise in Genesis 2 and 3 has made practically no impression, apparently, on the rest of the Old Testament, and where this theme of the garden of Eden is mentioned
later, the thought seems to go back to that mythical thinking
which lay behind the accounts in Genesis, and to see things from
the pagan viewpoint. The account of the 'garden of God' in
Ezekiel, as we have noticed, lacks the sober spirituality of the
Yahwist: it shows far less insight into the life of man with God,
yet for some reason it has had an extraordinary influence on
christian thinking. If we look again at the verses we are considering in Genesis and think of them in the light of *mystical
experience*— an experience which is actually the underlying
theme of all the Scriptures— we shall see here the very first
hint of that relationship into which God wished to draw the
human race: the relationship of love between God and man,
which is the *end* for which man was created, but into which, as
the Bible testifies, it is so difficult for him to enter.

I heard the sound of thy voice in the garden, and I was
afraid.

How vivid a description of the felt and realized presence of
God from which man in his weakness and frailty drew back in

alarm and hid himself, 'because I was naked'. With the nakedness he could cope— the external advance. But to that other *inner* advance to which God called him man was not yet ready to respond. He could not rise up to living with the burning love of God which for a moment flashed upon him. He realized his nakedness, and in his felt helplessness and weakness, he could not respond to the great Love that reached out to him. Again and again in the story of the Chosen People God calls to them, drawing them to Himself with yearning love, and repeatedly they draw back, in faithlessness and fear, until there comes the great culminating cry,

Jerusalem, Jerusalem, killing the prophets and stoning those that are sent to you. How often would I have gathered your children as a hen gathers her brood under her wings, and ye would not (St. Matt. 23:37).

Hiding himself from God, Adam could no longer live in Paradise. He had come to a turning point in life when he must advance, and there was no going back to the state of the childhood of our race. Had he been able to respond to the magnetic love of God, who can tell what the outcome might not have been? The Old Testament is the story of God's purpose slowly pursuing its way to an appointed end, but constantly baffled and thwarted by sin. Man's misery is due to his perpetual disloyalty to God, to his refusal to respond to the yearning love that draws him upwards.

Since God is life, wrote St. Basil, to be deprived of God is death. Adam, turning away from God merited death (Hom. Quod Deus non est auctor malorum P.G. 31,345 A).

Henceforth the human race was to live with a perpetual nostalgia in its heart for some unknown good of which it had somehow been deprived, and with a twist in its nature for which it sought in some way or another to account. Sin and death became man's portion, hatred and disunity were to dog the steps of the human race. God asked from man a response— He

called him to share in the divine life of the Trinity, to enter
into the fullness of that love which is the very essence of the Life
of God, who *is* Love.   Man might no longer simply live and
bask in the peace and plenty of Paradise; he must rise up and
enter into a life of *personal* relationship with his Creator.   Can
we be surprised that man at that initial stage of his new, higher
development shrank back from the bright beam of that love
when that great Mystical Doctor of the Church, St. John
of the Cross, described the reaction of christian saints and
mystics to the first touch of God in the soul as one of fear and
amazement? The touch of God, he said, though it is so gentle
and tender, is felt by the unpurified soul as a weight and a
burden.   The light, magnetic beam of God's love is almost
more than the mystic can at first endure, until he has been
made strong and steadfast by passive suffering.   St. John of the
Cross drew the comparison between this shining of God's love
on the soul with the shining of the full light of the sun on
diseased and sensitive eyes to which it brings pain and distress.

One of the greatest of the Old Testament mystics, the
prophet Isaiah, saw God's purpose of salvation as *preceding* his
purpose of creation.   His purpose from the first was that men
should 'look to him and be saved' (Is. 45:22).   Though this
was God's purpose from the beginning, and though He saw
this end from the very first, the goodness of His divine purpose
had to be revealed that men might co-operate and carry it
out intelligently and spiritually.   Yet this communication could
only be made slowly and gradually because the creature could
not take it in.   Only as certain chosen vessels were able to
receive God's self-revelation and surrender themselves to it, did
this become possible, and for mortal man to receive this divine
self-revelation was and is extraordinarily difficult.   From all
eternity, we believe, man was destined to share in the life
of God, but only very slowly could our frail, creaturely nature
respond to the divine purpose.

This brings us to the central core of the question we are
considering.   What is the real background, the cause, of that
'nostalgia' which has haunted the human race as far back as
we can trace, and still haunts it in our own day?   Professor

Eliade, one of the most brilliant writers of our time on primitive
and Eastern religious cultures, sees here something in the human
race that may be called a 'nostalgia for paradise', for that
condition which, in christian terms, we may call the state
'before the Fall'. Certainly we cannot set this possibility aside.
In fact, there is a sense in which it is undoubtedly true as far as
we can judge. In many religious traditions, which go very far
back in the history of religions, there are various techniques by
which this 'paradisal' state is sought for and apparently often
temporarily achieved. The aim is to transcend the natural
fallen state of man and for the space of the ecstasy achieved by
these techniques to return to or re-enter the paradisal condition
which, it is believed, was man's original condition. Now this
'natural' mysticism is something very different from the mysticism of the Bible— Jewish, Christian and Moslem mysticism—
which throughout is concerned with man's relationship with
God and his surrender to the divine will and the divine guidance,
and therefore involves a *divine encounter*, not simply the enjoy-
ment of some mystical condition. Man, at the moment which
in mythical and very vivid language the old Hebrew writer has
depicted so beautifully, failed to rise to that response which God's
love demanded of him. In the verses we are considering he
places before us something which always now belongs to the
human situation: God's call to man and man's acceptance or
refusal of that call. On the technical, scientific, material plane
man responded; in the spiritual sphere which at the same time
was opened up to his gaze, he failed to respond. He could no
longer return to the state of the spiritual childhood of our race
which was his in the garden of Paradise, while at the same time
he could not rise up to the call which came to him from God to
enter into a life of personal union with Him, which would have
meant that his development on the spiritual plane would have
kept pace with his development on the rational, material plane,
when the two would have corresponded, and humanity would
have developed on the lines which were planned for it in the
divine purpose of God. Therefore, outside the garden, yet
lacking the spiritual power to rise to intimacy with God, man
fell instead under the dominion of the fallen angels, and at the

same time brought the rest of creation, of which he was the spearhead, under the same evil power.

If we look at it in this way it seems to me that in these verses we find the keynote of all the Scriptures, both of the Old Testament and of the New. In the Bible, as indeed everywhere else, there is a very clearly defined tendency to something which is absolutely contrary to this 'nostalgia for Paradise': a *resistance* to the sacred, to God. This *resistance* we see to be at the very heart of the religious experience itself: it is placed before us by the Yahwist writer in his earliest chapters. The transcendent reality of the sacred at once attracts and repels: in face of it man is almost irresistibly attracted and almost as irresistibly repelled, terrified. This resistance is most clearly realized when man comes face to face with God, when God calls to him and demands of him a response, a self-committal which must be based on faith, for no man has seen God at any time. Yet to resist the sacred, to turn away from the approach of God, is a *flight from reality* (M. Eliade). This resistance may possibly be most clearly realized within the very innermost circles of the life of the Church, at the very heart of religion, for probably it is here that the supreme encounter between God and man will take place. History shows man to have a 'deeply rooted repugnance to abandoning himself totally to sacred experience as clearly as it shows his powerlessness to resign that experience wholly'. [11]

We are left with the question: is that nostalgia which appears to lie in the heart of the human race a nostalgia for a lost Paradise in which it once lived and which lies, as it were, buried in the vast subconscious of humanity? Or, on the other hand, is it a 'nostalgia' for that union with the Living God from which Adam turned away? Is it a dim response and yearning aroused by the hidden, magnetic Love of God, who never ceases to whisper to each soul 'Where art thou?', and is for ever drawing us to Himself in love? May not that electromagnetic power which we now know to be at work in the planetary system be a sign or a symbol that the same magnetic power is also at work in the world of the spirit?

---

[11] M. Eliade, *Patterns in Comparative Religion*, p. 460.

CHAPTER X

THE LAND FLOWING WITH MILK
AND HONEY

STRANGELY ENOUGH THE Hebrew hope was but little concerned with the idea of immortality which played so large a part in the mythical thought of the surrounding cultures. In the Oriental world-view, in Egypt and Mesopotamia, there were many extravagant notions about heaven as the home of departed spirits. There was a real 'mythical' geography of the heavenly bodies— the sun, the moon, and the Milky Way— which we shall find again in Greek thought. It was thought that souls travelled up to heaven on the third day, for in some traditions the souls of the departed were thought to hover around their bodies for three days after their death. There were conceptions of the various circles of heaven, which were connected with the planetary systems, and so on. The thought of the Old Testament in comparison with these views is sober and realistic. In fact, the thought of life after death appears almost to fall into the background, for here, in 'salvation history', a new thing had come into the world which, for the Hebrews, completely overshadowed everything else: God spoke to one man, and held out promises to him if he would only believe. Abraham believed the word of Yahweh, and salvation history began. The promise was of land and posterity, and these were to become the great hope of the wandering semitic tribesmen.

The Hebrews were not primarily concerned with immortality and life after death, but with this present life here, in this world, in which Yahweh spoke to them and took them under His protection. The nomad tribes of the mid-second millenium were promised possession of the land of Canaan— the 'land flowing with milk and honey'— and posterity which should be

as the 'sand of the sea for multitude'. The Israelites loved
life, which to them was a gift of God. Their ideal was to live
on inherited land, to have many sons, to see the fruit of their toil
and to share in the blessing of their people (R. Martin-
Achard). They were not, in the usually accepted sense,
mystics, seeking to lose themselves in God and to become
absorbed in Him. But throughout life in this world the true
Hebrew sees and meets God, for he believes that everything
comes to him from the hand of God: his is that 'I and Thou'
relationship with God which has in recent years been so well
brought out by Professor Buber. For him to *live* was more than
just to *be*. Life was a vital force, and Dr. Martin-Achard has
pointed out that the Hebrew word for life— *hayyim*— is plural in
force and stresses the intensive character of life: *hayah*, the singular form, has the force of 'muscular contraction'. Life involves
mobility, spontaneity and a real development; men must grow
and flourish and accomplish the end for which they were
created by God. Absence of movement was tantamount to a
negation of life, and therefore sickness, sleep and death were
regarded as enfeebled forms of life. [1] They saw life to be good,
and the supreme blessing on which all other blessings depended.
The ideal was to live to a good old age, and to be 'full of
days' (Gen. 35:29). There was a tradition that the ante-
diluvians lived longer than their descendants because they lived
closer to God.

> For thus saith the Lord unto the house of Israel, Seek ye me,
> and ye shall live (Amos 5:4).
> Seek good, and not evil, that ye may live: and so the Lord,
> the God of Hosts, shall be with you (Amos 5:14).

Nevertheless, for the believer this life is not the absolute good:
the supreme blessing is communion with God

> O God, thou art my God, cries the psalmist, my soul thirsteth
> for thee, my flesh also longeth after thee in a barren and dry

---

[1] To be awakened, to be healed, to be raised, means to recover every faculty,
and to be in possession of all the powers of life (R. Martin-Achard, *From Death
to Life*, p. 5).

land, where no water is. . . Thy loving kindness is better than
life. . . Because thou hast been my helper, therefore under the
shadow of thy wing will I rejoice (Ps. 63).

In the Wisdom literature *hayyim*— 'life', also means
blessing— the two are synonymous.   Suffering and failure,
loneliness and separation, sickness and sin, are all prejudicial
to that life which God has given us.   To live is to see the
light— that light which was the first creation of God.   So the
prophet Isaiah writes

> The people that walked in darkness have seen a great light;
> they that dwell in the land of the shadow of death, upon
> them hath the light shined (9:2).

Water, too, in the Old Testament, is a symbol and pledge of
life:

> The fear of the Lord is a fountain of life, to depart from the
> snares of death (Prov. 14:27).

The Old Testament speaks not only of the God of life, but of
the 'Living God', who reveals Himself as a *Person*.   He is
also the 'Holy One', and the life He gives is bound up with
holiness— a concept which developed very gradually but is yet
present throughout the Hebrew Scriptures, as it is, indeed, in
all religious thought everywhere and at all times.   The life
of the Chosen People did not depend on magic rites or on
mystical absorption, but on a *dialogue* with God, in which God
Himself took the initiative.   To live was to walk in His ways.
There was no question of *imagining* what the gods might be
like, but something completely different: to hear the voice
of the Lord as it was heard by the great figures in the Bible, and
to do His will as it was proclaimed through them.

The old Jewish 'credo' in Deuteronomy 26 begins with
salvation-history:

> A Syrian ready to perish was my father, and he went down
> into Egypt, and sojourned there with a few, and became there
> a nation, great, mighty and populous (Deut. 26:5).

As we have already seen, the Yahwist writer of the David-Solomon era added a 'primeval' history, based on the myths and traditions of the surrounding cultures.   In the primeval history of the Bible, however, there is a definite purpose: it shows God calling and leading His people— His 'Bride Israel'— in spite of her constant failures.   Adam, we are told, hearing God's voice in the garden 'hid himself', and therefore he was cast out of the garden, out of the sphere of God's protection, out of the place where he 'walked with God', since it was impossible for him to remain there after he had, as it were, turned his back on God.   Yet God made coverings of skins to clothe both Adam and Eve, showing that He still cared for them.   Cain, the murderer, though cursed for his sin, was yet given the divine protection, for the Lord set a mark upon him lest any, finding him, should kill him: the divine mercy was not altogether withdrawn.   There are various ways in which the story of Cain and Abel may be interpreted, but possibly it is simplest to see here, as a first result of Adam's sin, strife and hatred in family relationships.   Then, when the generations of men had become so wicked that God repented Himself of having created them and therefore sent the Flood to wipe them out, He yet saved righteous Noah and his family to begin a fresh posterity, and when the flood waters were abated gave the rainbow for a sign that this should never again come to pass.   Thus, over and over again God showed His will to love, and over and over again man ignored that love and fell away into sin and disobedience.   At last there came such discord— a discord illustrated by the story of the tower of Babel, and involving international strife— that it appeared as if even Yahweh Himself could do no more for man.   Then, at this point, when all seemed lost, salvation history began. Here primeval and sacred history dovetail.   In primeval history man's salvation is an open question.   Here we are given the answer to man's need: the call of Abraham, and his response.   The transition comes abruptly in Genesis 12:1-3:

> Now the Lord said unto Abram, Get thee out of thy country, and from thy kindred, and from thy father's house, unto a

land that I will shew thee: and I will make of thee a great
nation, and I will bless thee, and make thy name great: and
thou shalt be a blessing: and I will bless them that bless thee,
and curse him that curseth thee: and in thee shall all the
families of the earth be blessed.

God speaks to one individual man, here in this world, and
gives him amazing promises, but demands complete self-
committal.

We do not really know how this divine call came to
Abraham.   In Joshua 24:3 we are told

I took your father Abraham from the other side of the River,
and led him through all the land of Canaan, and multiplied
his seed, and gave him Isaac.

This probably took place during one of the great ethnic
movements of the second millenium. [2]

The Yahwist writer, whose work is predominant in Genesis,
describes with a wonderful clarity and simplicity the individual
scenes in his narrative.   He is one of the great psychologists
among the Biblical writers, and his work is one of the most
wonderful achievements of all time.   In his primeval history
the great problems of humanity are reviewed in the light of
divine revelation: he considers creation and nature, man and
wife, sin and suffering, family quarrels and international confusion.   The stories of Paradise and the Fall, of Cain, of Noah
and the Flood reveal God's merciful protection and forgiveness.
They form the necessary prelude to *salvation* history, which is a
story of wonderful, hidden guidance and dispensation, in which
we can detect 'the vigour of a discoverer's joy' (von Rad).
Both the Yahwist and the later Elohist begin with their own
self-understanding: their own life with God which sheds so
much light on the true life of the Chosen People.   Nevertheless,
this is not their only point of departure: the starting-point of
their narratives is in the traditions of their people, handed down

[2] S.H. Hooke, *Alpha and Omega*, p. 20.

through the centuries, and finally accumulated by them and made available for all men for all time.   What they do is to enlarge the *inner* events from 'a unique to a kind of *typical* occurrence' (von Rad).   They give us something universally valid.   The fact that God miraculously preserves the promise beyond human failure is *the* great fact of history for the Israelites.   In all these narratives there is a subtle spirituality.

In the story of Abraham we have a picture of the most intimate relations with God: so intimate, in fact, that we can but marvel that it should have been possible to transmit them to posterity.   Yet we must accept this record of a profound *personal* experience of God, and of this first response to God's search by which He could begin to heal the breach between God and man caused by Adam's sin.   Or, to put it differently, a way in which He might draw men to Himself in the Life of Love of the Blessed Trinity.   First, we must think of the wonderful response of faith which enabled Abraham to go out into the unknown in utter dependence on that divine command, which, it is well to remember, was heard by him alone.   He was subjected to severe tests and trials.   How could there be any truth in a promise that his seed should be as the 'sand of the sea for multitude' when his wife Sarah was childless in her old age?

When he heard the promise that a child would yet be born to Sarah Abraham laughed (Gen. 17:17).   At her age, surely not!   Yet it came to pass and the hope rose high.   Then the time came when God demanded the sacrifice of this precious child, this firstborn, this hope of all Israel in whom the promises must be fulfilled.   God had given beyond all hope and expectation, and then it appeared that he who had given so much insisted on taking it away.   Here was a test of almost inconceivable difficulty, yet the divine voice had again spoken to Abraham, and since his whole life and hope was committed to that guiding voice heard in the depths of his being and followed with unswerving loyalty, that voice must again be obeyed in this, as in all else.   Otherwise his whole life was a complete mistake, and his hope groundless.   If the voice of God was true when he heard it before— and he had no reason to doubt that—

then it must be believed again, for the 'inner' voice had
become the guiding principle of this wandering tribesman in
those far off days.   Here is an account of marvellous clarity
and depth, showing a rich, full interior life, of familiar intercourse between this one man and his God.   It reveals with
immense clarity the spiritual genius of the Hebrew people.
The sacrifice, as we know, was not required, but the faith of
God's chosen witness had proved sufficient for all things.

Though the other promise, that of the land of Canaan, the
'land flowing with milk and honey', was not fulfilled in
Abraham's lifetime, nor for a long time to come, yet this
patriarch who forsook all at the divine command was not
wholly unrewarded even in this respect, and the promise did
not utterly fail.   Before his death he was able to purchase a
field of the sons of Heth (Gen. 25:10), and in that field both he
and Sarah his wife were buried.   One tiny spot of the promised
land was theirs, and therefore they did not lie, in death, in
Hittite soil, but in one small corner of that promised land which
was their very own.   In this grave, with Abraham, was buried
not only Sarah, but also Isaac and Rebekah, his wife, Leah
(Gen. 49:31) and finally Jacob:

> His sons carried him into the land of Canaan, and buried him
> in the cave of the field of Machpelah, which Abraham bought
> with the field for a possession of a burying place (Gen. 50:
> 13).

Here there is an indirect prophecy of great value: in a sense
it foreshadows the benefits of the salvation which is in Christ.
It is, as it were, a preview of our relationship to the saving
benefits of our faith, of the 'new life' *in Christ* into which
we all die.   The early Fathers of the Church regarded Christ
as the 'promised land', in whom all the promises were actually
fulfilled, and in the Church in Rome during the earlier centuries
a chalice of milk and honey was administered to the newly-
baptized at the Baptismal Eucharist in addition to the chalice
of wine and water, signifying that they were now come to the
true promised land— that land 'flowing with milk and honey,

— the true Paradise of God for which the heart of man has ever yearned.   So, says St. Paul, ' we are buried with Christ in baptism': into that portion of the promised land which is ours in this life.

The secret things belong unto the Lord our God: but those things which are revealed belong unto us and to our children for ever (Deut. 29:29).

CHAPTER XI

JACOB'S LADDER

THE BIBLICAL WRITER known as the Elohist, who wrote some two centuries later than the Yahwist, has a somewhat different approach to his material. His work does not appear till the Abraham narratives. The first eleven chapters of Genesis are the work of the Yahwist and the 'Priestly' writer, who was the latest of the three and in whose work the traditional religious teaching of the Hebrew people, handed down through the centuries, is clearly evident. The Elohist's work only appears with the beginning of 'salvation history'. In a sense the first eleven chapters are also written from the standpoint of salvation history: they are not an account of how the world was made, but rather the 'pillars' on which the later salvation history is built. In the early books of the Bible it is not so much the soul of man or his destiny that is the main interest, but the fact of the 'Living God' and all the wonders He performs. These books give us a picture of life in this world in which the moving and all-important power is the good God. The Israelites could not conceive of a development of the soul without the body: the two were for them of equal importance. Neither did they think of God as aloof and apart from this world of men, but as intervening in their affairs, as most deeply interested and concerned with what befell them. This world they knew to be God's world, His creation, even as they knew themselves to be His people, His Chosen, His beloved, the 'apple of his eye'.

Miracles, in their more spectacular aspect, receive more emphasis with the Elohist than they do in the Yahwist's simple and lucid writings. His narratives have more of the old folklore tradition, and have not on the whole been spiritualized to the same degree as those of the earlier writer. Nevertheless, he has his own definite theological contribution to make, by which the earlier tradition is enriched.   One or two of his characteristics may be mentioned, as they are of some interest. In the first place, the sense of that immediate intimacy between God and man on earth which is so prominent in the earlier writer, is strictly limited.   Usually it is the 'angel' of the Lord rather than God Himself who appears and speaks to man.   He calls down, as it were, from Heaven, and no longer walks this earth.   The whole thought is more imbued with the ' otherness ' of God, of His transcendence and His holiness.   The writer may actually have been in contact with the thought of the 8th century prophet Isaiah and would thus have been influenced by that conception of God's holiness which is one of the keynotes of the Isaianic literature.   This may also account for his second characteristic: the importance he gives to the prophet and his office.   He obviously wrote in the period of the great writing prophets, and his emphasis on the 'prophetic' side is so strong that we may even conjecture that he wrote from within prophetic circles.   His work is predominant in the book of Exodus, as the Yahwist's is in Genesis. Many ages and traditions lie behind their monumental work. They see God's leading in the facts of history as well as in the ordinary course of human life; not only in the sacred things, but also in the profane.   Everywhere it is a story of wonderful divine guidance and protection.   These two writers mention the smallest details.   They show the conflicts and temptations into which their characters fell, and the mistakes they made, even at those all-important moments when the divine message came to them.   Another aspect of the Elohist's approach is the importance he attaches to *dreams*, which, since God now no longer walks in familiar intercourse with men in this world, become the sphere where God's revelation and His message come to men.   So we find God saying to Abimelech in a dream

> Yea, I know that thou didst this in the integrity of thine heart; for I also witheld thee from sinning against me: Therefore I suffered thee not to touch her (Sarah).   Now therefore restore the man his wife: for he is a prophet, and he shall pray for thee, and thou shalt live (Gen. 20:6, 7).

Here we find two of this writer's characteristics combined: the message coming in a dream and the importance of the prophetic office. Yet in some cases even these dreams have to be interpreted through a special gift and enablement of God, and do not of necessity bring the recipient into direct contact with the divine. This lack of immediate intimacy with God is, however, to some extent balanced by the word and message of the prophets. 'Speak thou with us' said the people to Moses, 'and we will hear; but let not God speak with us, lest we die' (Exodus 20:19).

These stories in the early books of the Bible may best be described as 'sagas'. Now sagas are the form in which a people relate their own history, and these 'historical' sagas therefore relate events on a more spiritual plane than profane history can possibly do. [1] They tell of experience of a singular divine guidance, and reveal something that may best be described as ' becoming mature in the mysteries of life '. They are, in fact, a 'history with God' (von Rad.). Thus the saga has a wonderful transparency and depth of its own; it returns to the past, but is also, at the same time, a contingent act of God. In the Old Testament sagas there is no attempt to idealize the characters, as is the case in most other sagas of national folklore, where the heroes are held up for the emulation of the people. Instead we find men who are sinners, weak and afraid, often failing and then rising up out of their failures in God's strength. Jacob, and Moses, and David, the ideal king, are fallible, and we wonder how, with their deeds which now seem to us so far from ideal, they could have been the chosen of God. Clearly the Old Testament sagas are not concerned with idealizing men; the whole thought is concentrated on God, and His wonderful providence. Everywhere in these narratives God is the *inner*, true subject. Men are never important for their own sakes. Nevertheless, however important the theological element is here, it is never the *only* element: the 'historical' moment is always preserved.

---

[1] 'It is a view and interpretation of that which once was, but of a past event that is secretly present and decisive for the present... It is an *inner* history, one that takes place on a higher level, a story of inner events.' (von Rad, *Genesis*, ad loc.)

Possibly the best known of all the dreams recorded in the Bible is that of Jacob's ladder. It is thought that this passage— Genesis 28:10-22— is the joint work of both our writers: the Yahwist and the Elohist. Verses 10-12 are the work of the Elohist, as well as verses 17-22, with the exception of verse 19. Verses 13-16 and verse 19 are attributed to the Yahwist. The two views or approaches we have mentioned are here closely intermingled. Characteristically the Elohist tells us that Jacob, going towards Haran, came to a certain place and lay down to sleep, putting a stone for his pillow, and there he dreamed a dream in which he beheld 'a ladder set up on earth and the top of it reached to heaven; and behold the angels of God ascending and descending upon it'. Characteristically, too, the Yahwist adds:

> And, behold, the Lord God stood above it, and said, I am the Lord God of Abraham, thy father, and the God of Isaac: the land whereon thou liest, to thee will I give it, and to thy seed; and thy seed shall be as the dust of the earth, and thou shalt spread abroad to the west and to the east, and to the north and to the south: and in thee and in thy seed shall all the families of the earth be blessed. And, behold, I am with thee, and will keep thee in all places whither thou goest, and will bring thee again to this land; for I will not leave thee, until I have done that which I have spoken to thee of.

And Jacob, awaking out of his sleep, said 'Surely the Lord was in this place, and I knew it not.' Again the Elohist takes up the story:

> And he was afraid, and said, How dreadful is this place! This is none other but the house of God and the gate of heaven.

The 'gate of heaven' refers to that narrow place in which, in the thought of the ancients, all intercourse between earth and heaven took place. Between these two spheres the angels of God come and go continually, fulfilling God's commands or supervising what is done here below. In Job, quite a late book, the Lord says to Satan, 'Whence comest thou?'

Then Satan answered the Lord, and said, From going to and fro through the earth (Job 1:7).

Again, in Zechariah's first vision, the angel gives answer to his question,

These are they whom the Lord hath sent to walk to and fro through the earth (Zech. 1: 10).

We must not picture the ladder in this vision as something which we now call a ladder in the ordinary sense of the word, for that would not have been wide enough for the angels to pass one another upon it as they went swiftly to and fro about their business. The Hebrew word refers rather to a kind of 'stairlike pavement'. [1] In the ancient oriental view a distinction was made between the earthly place of God's appearing and His actual dwelling-place. On the great Babylonian towers the 'dwelling-place' of the god was the uppermost chamber, while below on the ground was the place where the god appeared, and from top to bottom of this great building was a long ramp, its characteristic mark. The 'ziqqurat', too, the tower of the temple, was considered in ancient Babylonia as the bond between earth and heaven: a 'centre' where men might meet with God. So here Jacob probably saw a 'ziqqurat' or wide ramp, with the angels going up and down upon it. It was a figure Jesus Himself was to use:

Hereafter ye shall see heaven open, and the angels of God ascending and descending upon the Son of Man (John 1: 51).

Here, however, it is no longer the 'ladder' or 'ziqqurat' upon which the angels go up and down, but Christ himself: he is the one way between earth and heaven, he *himself* is the *centre* where men may come to God and to heaven. Moreover,

[1] Ibid., p. 279.

as St. Augustine was to point out, he is not the way to something other than himself: Christ is not only the *way*, but also the *end* to which that way leads.

The experience of this night meant much more than a consoling dream to the patriarch, for here something *happened*, there had been a revelation from God, and henceforth that place was 'holy ground' :

Surely the Lord is in this place, and I knew it not.

And he called that place Bethel, which means the 'house of God'. Jacob was overcome with awe and wonder, and we should now say that he had experienced a mystic vision, but the old Hebrew writer simply says he had a dream. After all, it is scarcely surprising that in the olden days the two were indistinguishable; perhaps, in fact, their understanding of these things had not yet come to discern the difference between them. 'And I knew it not'— not at the time, but only later when he came to himself did he know with absolute conviction that he had been with God and God with him, and that is, according to St. Theresa of Avila, a true mark of mystical experience. We may note, too, that it is no longer the 'gate of Paradise', or the entrance to the Garden of Eden, but the 'gate of heaven', and the presence of God Himself, for 'Behold the Lord stood above' the ladder. Clearly we have here a very ancient tradition, for it is all bound up with the promise made to Abraham: the blessing of posterity and lands, and the constant divine protection. Here, too, the two ways to God are brought together: the simple, easy way— God holding His children in His hand and caring for them—and that other way of awe and wonder which acknowledges the transcendence of the all-holy God who has drawn so close to His Servant: 'the God of Jacob, our father'.

Here, too, is an illustration of that ambivalent feeling of attraction and repulsion which Professor Eliade has seen to be so characteristic of all 'ladder' symbolism, and which makes that symbolism so rich and interesting. It gives expression to that persistent 'motif' of passing from one mode of being to another, of breaking through the different planes of being. Apparently modern psychoanalytical investigation has shown conclusively that this symbolism belongs

> to the archaic content of the human psyche and is not a historical creation, nor an innovation dating from a certain historical moment. [3]

This is because the image of a ladder or a stairway, of the very act of climbing or ascending, is symbolic of the approach towards *absolute reality*, and the approach to this reality produces in the ordinary human being a feeling both of fear and of joy, of attraction and of repulsion. 'How dreadful is this place!' 'The symbolism of stairs or of a ladder contains the ideas of sanctification, of death, love and deliverance.' [4] It means the passing from unreality to that which is utterly *real* and *true*. Now this applies also to all the 'tree' symbolisms, because, as we have seen, they are set up at a 'centre', which makes possible a connection between one mode of being and another. In the mystical literature of Christianity, as in many other religious cultural traditions, we find this formula of the 'mystic ladder', or the 'ladder of perfection', by which the mystic seeks to come closer to God. In a treatise entitled 'The Ladder of Paradise', written by St. John Climacus about the beginning of the 7th century A.D., and based on the story of Jacob's Ladder in Genesis, we see very clearly how the way of salvation and fellowship with God was conceived in the spiritual circles of Mount Sinai, where it was written. The monks there sought always to mount higher and higher on the heavenly ladder by isolation and contemplation. They called it the ladder of 'Eros', the aspiring love of God. Gradually the writer takes us step by step up the heavenly way of devotion. The first 26 steps of the ladder deal with the overcoming of vices, while the last four of the thirty steps deal with the virtues: solitude, prayer, dispassion and love. The monks aimed at reaching such rest or 'apathy' as is a reflection of

---

[3] M. Eliade, *Images and Symbols*, p. 50.
[4] A. Nygren, *Agape and Eros*, Part 2, vol. 2 (SPCK. 1939), p. 377.

God's own rest.   Only those who lived lives of isolation as hermits could hope to attain this end, and when they did reach it they had heaven in their hearts.   Yet there was still one stage left which they could not attain by their own efforts or devotion. At the top of Jacob's ladder stood God Himself, and for full fellowship with Him man must attain to that divine *Agape* which is a pure gift of God.   On the top of the *Eros* ladder *Agape* is enthroned, for God Himself is Agape, and He alone can bestow it upon his children.   The last chapter— the last rung of the ladder— speaks not of Eros but of Agape: God's self-giving love which is so clearly revealed in the Gospel of Christ. This last step cannot be reached by the monk's own efforts; it is something God alone can give of His free bounty when and where He wills.

'I long to know how Jacob saw thee fixed above the ladder' says Climacus, 'Satisfy my desire, tell me, what are the means to such an ascent?'   God answers:

> 'On the top of the ladder I have established myself, as my great initiate said: and now there remain faith, hope, love— these three; but the greatest of all is love'. [5]

In the refectory of the monastery of the Great Lavra on Mount Athos this 'Ladder' is depicted in the frescoes which adorn it.   This fresco is known as 'The Ladder of the Spirit', but apparently the monks do not know its real meaning, for they have but little interest in books and learning.   They know, however, that the ladder goes up 'from the monastery to our Lord'.   One fresco shows a monk on the topmost step and Christ holding out his hand to him and crowning him with a wreath.   Another depicts a monk nearly at the top being assisted by an angel, while a third shows an unfortunate monk being snatched down by a devil.   From these frescoes the un-learned come to grasp what they are unable to gather from books.

One of the outstanding themes of the Old Testament is that of the divine approach to man.   Here it is God rather than man

---

[5] St. John Climacus, (E.T.), *The Ladder of Divine Ascent*, pp. 265, 266. Faber & Faber, 1959.

who is the seeker. This is brought out very clearly in placing the divine approach during the night, often in dreams. The child Samuel was called by the Lord and answered 'Here I am', thinking it was the aged Eli who had called him. He ran in to the old man and said 'Thou didst call me', but Eli denied having done this and sent the child back to bed. Again the Lord called 'Samuel', and again he went to Eli and was sent to lie down once more. When it happened a third time 'Eli perceived that the Lord had called the child' (1 Sam. 3:8). Therefore he said to him this time, 'Go, lie down: and it shall be, if he call thee, that thou shalt say, Speak, Lord; for thy servant heareth'. And the Lord came and stood and called again, and then was able to reveal to Samuel what He was about to do. What he revealed was something far from the child's thoughts, and he feared to tell Eli the message that had been given him. How realistic it all is, this ancient narrative; how utterly devoid of any possibility of wishful thinking or self-persuasion. On the other hand the longing for union with God is frequently expressed in the psalms:

O God, thou art my God; early will I seek thee: my soul thirsteth for thee, and my flesh longeth for thee in a dry and thirsty land, where no water is;...
My soul shall be satisfied as with marrow and fatness; and my mouth shall praise thee with joyful lips; when I remember thee upon my bed, and meditate on thee in the night watches. Because thou hast been my help, therefore under the shadow of thy wings will I rejoice' (Ps. 63:5-7).
As the hart panteth after the water brooks, so panteth my soul after thee, O God (Ps. 42:1).

Yet this is surely only the other side of the same truth: the prevenient grace of God, drawing man to Himself hiddenly as well as revealing Himself in vision and prophecy. Man could not long for God, for the divine union, had not God in some measure already found him and elicited the response of yearning love to His own loving approach: 'We love him because he first loved us' (1 Jn. 4:19).

CHAPTER XII

EDEN AND JERUSALEM

Among the 'mythical' passages in the Old Testament there are a number which bear on the *paradise* motif. The prophets of Israel frequently employed this mythical language in proclaiming the future. Amos, for example, says:

> Behold, the days come, saith the Lord, that the ploughman shall overtake the reaper, and the treader of grapes him that soweth seed: and the mountains shall drop sweet (or new) wine, and all the hills shall melt.
> And I will bring again the captivity of my people Israel, and they shall build the waste cities, and inhabit them; and they shall plant vineyards, and drink the wine thereof; they shall also make gardens, and eat the fruit of them (Amos 9:13-14).

Isaiah speaks of the wilderness becoming a fruitful field, and fruit trees in such number that they form a forest:

> Until the spirit be poured upon us from on high, and the wilderness be a fruitful field, and the fruitful field be counted as a forest... Then judgment shall dwell in the wilderness, and righteousness remain in the fruitful field. And the work of righteousness shall be peace: and the effect of righteousness peace and assurance for ever (Is. 32:15-17).

Here the prophet combines with his mythical language some of the most characteristic aspects of his teaching: the righteousness and peace which are promised by God to His people and which He longs to bestow upon them if they will only walk in His ways.

The Old Testament does not envisage the reign of the Messiah as resting on the original, primeval innocence and perfection. It is concerned above all with God's self-revelation to His people in their history here in this world, and with His purpose for them, for the Israelites have known *by experience* God's tender, fatherly care for them, and the wonder of his simple, humble love outweighs all other considerations and mythical ideas. The thought of resurrection seldom appears, but the prophets base their hopes on God's justice, on the conviction that he will vindicate those who have put their trust in him, a thought which comes very much to the fore in the Maccabean struggle, when martyrdom for their faith first arises. Where passages which may be construed as messianic prophecies combine this idea with mythical, pictorial language, the form of the passage goes back behind the Yahwist to an older mythical tradition, which was part of the folklore of many nations, who shared the dream of a past golden age. In these primitive stories there was also often a 'divine Helper', or an 'ideal king'. Osiris, for example, was distinguished in Egypt because of the great advantages that accrued to the people of that land during his reign. He gathered them together into organized societies, and taught them the fundamentals of agriculture, instructing them in the use of wheat. He also had them taught the art of weaving their own clothes. He abolished cannibalism. His sister and wife, Isis, helped him with this work and founded the marriage tie and family life. Clearly, then, Osiris was a benefactor to his people. Not content, however, with the progress of his own subjects and with their happiness, he wished to spread those benefits all over the world, and for this purpose set forth to bring men of all nations into submission by persuasion and gentleness. Here was a real 'golden age' of the past. [1]

In some of the early chapters of Isaiah the prophet holds out promises of universal peace. In 9:6 there is a list of mysterious names which have behind them men's agelong dreams, in which the ideal king, or shepherd, or gardener will come and will care for his own:

---

[1] G. Nagel, 'The Mysteries of Osiris in Ancient Egypt' in Eranos Yearbook II, *The Mysteries.*

Unto us a child is born, unto us a son is given: and the
government shall be upon his shoulder: and his name shall
be called, Wonderful, Counsellor, The mighty God, The
everlasting Father, the Prince of Peace.

In Isaiah 4:2 the soil is envisaged as supernaturally fertile
without the exaggerated descriptions which we find in the early
pagan myths.   The idea of a supernaturally fruitful earth, of
water poured on the parched ground, of the wilderness
becoming fertile, mountains levelled and valleys lifted up, is
found all through the Old Testament period, right up to
Rabbinic times.   Though later some of these descriptions again
became fantastic they do not become so in the canonical
writings, which are always restrained in spite of their lyrical
beauty, as in chapter 35 of Isaiah:

> The desert shall rejoice and blossom as the rose, it shall
> blossom abundantly, and rejoice even with joy and singing:
> the glory of Lebanon shall be given unto it, the excellency of
> Carmel and Sharon, they shall see the glory of the Lord,
> and the excellency of our God... Say to them that are of a
> fearful heart, Be strong, fear not: behold, your God will come
> with vengeance, even God with a recompense; he will come
> and save you.   Then the eyes of the blind shall be opened,
> and the ears of the deaf shall be unstopped.   Then shall the
> lame man leap as an hart, and the tongue of the dumb sing: for
> in the wilderness shall waters break out, and streams in the
> desert... An highway shall be there, and a way, and it shall
> be called The way of holiness; the unclean shall not pass over
> it: but it shall be for those: the wayfaring men, though fools,
> shall not err therein. No lion shall be there, nor any ravenous
> beast shall go up thereon... but the redeemed shall walk
> there: and the ransomed of the Lord shall return, and come to
> Zion with songs and everlasting joy upon their heads: they
> shall obtain joy and gladness, and sorrow and sighing shall flee
> away.

Here all the typical paradisal language is employed and
intermingled with visions of the earth as it shall be in the
coming messianic age.   In the New Testament teaching the

coming of the Saviour brings with it a restoration of the
original plan of creation, of a restored Paradise, of a second
Adam and a second Eve. As Jesus went about Galilee in the
years of his ministry it must have seemed to many that here the
prophecy of Isaiah was at last fulfilled:

> Jesus went about all Galilee, teaching in their synagogues and
> preaching the gospel of the kingdom, and healing all manner
> of sickness and all manner of disease among the people. And
> his fame went throughout all Syria: and they brought unto
> him all sick people that were taken with divers diseases and
> torments, and those which were possessed with devils, and
> those that were lunatick, and those that had the palsy: and he
> healed them (St. Matt. 4:23-4).

In the New Testament, indeed, the paradisal idea is central,
and the thought of the garden of Eden is brought into prom-
inence.   The thought is that of a new heaven and a new earth
which are different from the present order.   Though the Old
Testament does not envisage another world and another life,
the fundamental ideas are there to be developed at the coming
of the Messiah, who is, in Himself, the Kingdom of God:

> I am come that they may have life, and that they may have it
> more abundantly (St. John 10:10).

In a famous passage Isaiah combines his own prophetic
outlook with mythical language, weaving the two together
very skilfully, so that the mythical passage simply becomes a
description of the earth as it will be in the time to which he
looks forward at the coming of the Messiah:

> There shall come forth a rod out of the stem of Jesse, and
> a Branch shall grow out of his roots: and the spirit of the Lord
> shall rest upon him, the spirit of wisdom and understanding,
> the spirit of counsel and might, the spirit of knowledge and of
> the fear of the Lord: and shall make him of quick
> understanding in the fear of the Lord... and righteousness
> shall be the girdle of his loins, and faithfulness the girdle of
> his reins (Is. 11:1-5).

This is typical of the theology of the prophet, in fact, verse 2 is thought to have formed the basis for the idea of the seven-fold gifts of the Holy Spirit. Yet verses 6-8 bring us into an entirely different atmosphere, employing the language of myth, forming practically a counterpart to the Dilmun of early Mesopotamian mythology:

> The wolf shall dwell with the lamb, and the leopard shall lie down with the kid; and the calf and the young lion and the fatling together; and a little child shall lead them. And the cow and the bear shall feed; their young ones shall lie down together: and the lion shall eat straw like the ox. And the sucking child shall play on the hole of the asp, and the weaned child shall put his hand on the cockatrice den.

Verse 9 is again typical of Isaiah:

> They shall not hurt or destroy in all my holy mountain: for the earth shall be full of the knowledge of the Lord, as the waters cover the sea.

Here the sober, prophetic teaching contains the mythical passage with perfect ease.

Joel, too, speaks of mountains dripping with sweetness and hills flowing with milk:

> And it shall come to pass in that day, that the mountains shall drop new wine, and the hills shall flow with milk, and all the rivers of Judah shall flow with waters, and a fountain shall come forth out of the house of the Lord, and shall water the valley of Shittim (Joel 3:18).

This resembles the language of Persian mythology, but in the Bible it serves as a colourful description of the coming trans-formation of the world. Thus these passages lose their mythical connotation and become a description of a world which transcends the senses, that world which can only be conveyed to us under images and symbols, for

Since the beginning of the world men have not heard, nor
perceived by the ear, neither hath the eye seen, O God, beside
thee, what he hath prepared for him that waiteth for him
(Is. 64:4).

The Deutero-Isaiah promises that

The Lord shall comfort Zion: he will comfort all her waste
places; and he will make her wilderness like Eden, and her
desert like the garden of the Lord: joy and gladness shall be
found therein, and thanksgiving and the voice of melody
(Is. 51:3).

The people shall have the fulfilment of all their paradisal
desires:

Thus saith the Lord, thy Redeemer, the Holy One of Israel;
I am the Lord thy God... which leadeth thee by the way
thou shouldest go. O that thou hadst hearkened unto my
commandments! then had thy peace been as a river, and thy
righteousness as the waves of the sea: thy seed also had been
as the sand... tell this, utter it even to the ends of the earth,
The Lord hath redeemed his servant Jacob (Is. 48:17ff).

Since God had provided his people with water in the
wilderness, and had even caused water to flow out of the
rock for them, the prophet is convinced that He will also
in the future provide abundant water for their needs. The four
streams of Genesis testify to the goodness of God who wishes
thereby to fertilize the whole earth and make it habitable.
Thus it is possible to believe that God will renew his miracle
of the desert:

They thirsted not when he led them through the deserts: he
caused the water to flow out of the rock for them: he clave the
rock also, and the waters gushed out (Is. 48:21).

Their eschatology affirmed that in future times there would
be abundance of water and consequent fertility. This thought

is especially evident in the prophetic vision of a garden of Eden around Jerusalem, something which does not seem to them to be beyond the bounds of possibility:

And they shall say, This land that was desolate is become like the garden of Eden; and the waste and desolate and ruined cities are become fenced and inhabited (Ezek. 36:35).

By bringing together the origin of the world and their visions of the future blessedness the prophets saw the intervention of God in the coming Messianic age as a real *re-creation*, a fresh beginning of history. This return to the facts of the original creation we have seen to be one of the characteristics of primitive mythical thought, which combined with this idea the hope that the 'end' would be as the 'beginning': the *urzeit-endzeit* pattern. This is actually something we find in all spheres of life at all times. This idea of a fresh beginning is found in the celebration of the New Year, seeing it as a re-creation, an entirely fresh start, holding out possibilities of we know not what. Again, in moving from one home to another a new life is, in a sense begun, and we enter on a fresh venture, holding for us we know not what of future happiness or of loss. Our birthdays, too, hold for us as individuals a special portent which to children seems something very vital and important, for a birthday marks a definite stage in the process of growing up to maturity and a full share in the life of the world. This importance of fresh beginnings is, to a very great extent, one of the marks of our 'nostalgia for Paradise'.

One of the greatest mystics of the Old Testament, the prophet Isaiah, who, in his vision of the holiness of God heard that Trisagion which has sounded down the ages: 'Holy, holy, holy, is the Lord of Hosts: the whole earth is full of his glory ' (Is. 6:3), though he sometimes uses the language of ancient myth and folklore, transfers the centre of his thought from 'Paradise' as the 'garden' or Eden, to the *city*— Jerusalem or Zion. Thereafter Jerusalem becomes *par excellence* the *centre*: the place where God and man meet. Zion, or Jerusalem, is exalted to Paradise:

The word that Isaiah the son of Amos saw concerning Judah and Jerusalem.

And it shall come to pass in the last days, that the mountain of the Lord's house shall be established in the top of the mountains, and shall be exalted above the hills; and all nations shall flow unto it.

And many people shall go and say, Come ye, and let us go up to the mountain of the Lord, to the house of the God of Jacob; and he will teach us of his ways, and we will walk in his paths: for out of Zion shall go forth the law, and the word of the Lord from Jerusalem (Is. 2:1-3).

In a lovely passage he speaks of the Lord defending Jerusalem 'as birds flying'

As birds flying will the Lord of Hosts defend Jerusalem; defending also he will deliver it; and passing over he will preserve it (31:5).

He then goes on to speak of the blessings of the new kingdom:

A king shall reign in righteousness, and princes shall rule in judgment. And a man shall be as an hiding place from the wind, and a covert from the tempest; as rivers of water in a dry place, as the shadow of a great rock in a weary land. And the eyes of them that see shall not be dim, and the ears of them that hear shall hearken (32:1-3).

From the time of Josiah onwards Jerusalem was the only sanctuary in the land, and even in Solomon's time pilgrimages were made to it from all over Israel. Zechariah pictures the mountainous country of Judea sinking to the level of the Dead Sea (1,200 feet below sea level) from six miles nort hof Jerusalem to Rimmon, thirty-five miles to the south west, while the city Jerusalem itself remains at its elevation of about 2,500 feet above sea level:

All the land shall be turned as a plain from Geba to Rimmon south of Jerusalem: and it shall be lifted up, and inhabited in her place.. and men shall dwell in it, and there shall be no more utter desolation: but Jerusalem shall be inhabited (Zech: 14:10-11).

Jerusalem, surrounded by its walls, will thus stand out as an immense rocky pinnacle, rising up from the surrounding plain, really 'exalted among the hills'. In the coming Messianic age Jerusalem is pictured as the true centre to which all the nations shall flow, even as she is already the centre of Israel's unity. During the Exile the hearts of the Hebrew people longed and yearned for their beloved city:

By the waters of Babylon we sat down and wept, when we remembered thee, O Zion (Ps. 137:1).

When the Lord turned again the captivity of Zion, we were like unto them that dream. Then was our mouth filled with laughter, and our tongue with joy (Ps. 126:1-2).

After the return from Exile Jerusalem became more and more the centre and the gathering-point of both the Israelites and the gentiles:

Yea, many peoples and strong nations shall come to seek the Lord of hosts in Jerusalem, and to pray before the Lord (Zech. 8:22).

The conception of a spiritual Centre towards which all men would be drawn is retained and transformed in the actual fulfilment in Christ:

I, if I be lifted up from the earth, will draw all men unto me (Jn. 12:32).

The centre of unity is no longer the Temple but the Messiah Himself, the Incarnate Word, in whom all the prophecies have their fulfilment.

Ezekiel, who was given visions of a temple which was never to be built, saw the 'holy waters' flowing no longer from the Garden of Eden but from under the Temple, which was built on that primeval rock beneath which the *tehôm*— the deep waters of the underworld— were to be found. These waters finally become a river, running between banks bordered with trees, and

> These waters issue forth toward the eastern region, and shall go down into the Arabah: and they shall go toward the sea; into the sea shall the waters go which were made to issue forth; and the waters shall be healed. And it shall come to pass, that every living creature that swarmeth, in every place whither the rivers come, shall live... everything shall live whithersoever the river cometh (Ezek. 47:8-9 R.S.V.).

The Trito-Isaiah dwells much on the thought of Jerusalem and its blessedness:

> For Zion's sake I will not hold my peace, and for Jerusalem's sake I will not rest, until the righteousness thereof go forth as brightness, and the salvation thereof as a lamp that burneth... As a young man marrieth a maiden so shall thy sons marry thee: and as the bridegroom rejoiceth over the bride, so shall thy God rejoice over thee... Ye that make mention of the Lord keep not silence, and give him no rest, till he establish, and till he make Jerusalem a praise on the earth(Is. 62:1-7).

'Rejoice ye with Jerusalem, and be glad with her, all ye that love her' (66:10).

Later Judaism exalted this picture of the idealized Jerusalem to heaven. The destiny of the earthly and heavenly Jerusalem is linked together, for the heavenly Jerusalem came to be regarded as pre-existent. There the new generations shall find perfect happiness, and the just shall go there after death:

> The saints will rest in Eden, the just shall rejoice over Jerusalem (T. Dan. V. 12).

In the apocalypses the idea of the earthly Jerusalem recedes. St. Paul speaks of the difference between the two Jerusalems— the earthly and the heavenly— in Galatians 4:22ff, and lays stress on the loftiness of the new, heavenly Jerusalem, which is free, and 'the mother of us all'. Philo says:

> The city of God is called in Hebrew Jerusalem and its name when translated is 'vision of peace'.

The writer of the Epistle to the Hebrews tells those he addresses that they have here 'no continuing city', but that they seek one to come (Heb. 13:14):

> But ye are come unto mount Sion, and unto the city of the living God, the heavenly Jerusalem, and to an innumerable company of angels, to the general assembly and church of the firstborn, which are written in heaven, and to God the judge of all, and to the spirits of just men made perfect, and to Jesus the mediator of the new covenant (Heb. 12:22).

Finally, in the great Christian Apocalypse, blessed John the Seer sees

> The holy city, new Jerusalem, coming down from God out of heaven, as a bride adorned for her husband.

and hears a great voice cry

> Behold the tabernacle of God is with men, and he will dwell with them, and they shall be his people, and God himself shall be with them and be their God. And God shall wipe away all tears from their eyes; and there shall be no more death, neither sorrow, nor crying, nor any more pain; for the former things are passed away... Even so, come, Lord Jesus.

CHAPTER XIII

THE GREEK MYSTERIES AND
THEIR SECRET

AMONG THE GREAT religions of salvation which seek, as it
were, to 'save' mankind from some threatened catastrophe,
to preserve some precious principle which must not die and
which is yet constantly threatened with extinction, we must
place the 'Mystery' religions of Asia Minor, Greece and Syria:
Buddhism and the philosophy of the Indian Upanishads.
Very briefly, therefore, we will consider some of the Greek
Mystery cults and then glance at the religious thought of the
Far Eastern cultures. These *salvation* religions, which find
their culmination in Christianity, are of very great interest
to psychologists, for here it is clear that, as human consciousness develops, it strives for the supernatural life. [1]

Both Greek and Indian philosophy grew up under the
influence of the Mysteries, though they developed on very
different lines. In the Mediterranean basin and in western
Asia the religions of salvation had rites of initiation which
assured their adherents of immortality. In India, on the other
hand, where was no fear of death but rather of the 'wheel of
life', of perpetual transmigration, and of rebirth after each
death in this world, the philosophies, in common with that of
Buddhism, showed a way of escape from the miseries of life.
These all emerged at about the same time as the writing
prophets of Israel, that is, during the eight centuries before
Christ. There was at this time a tremendous religious and

---

[1] The element of the irrational, attested by the need for revelation or by
secret initiation, is a clear indication that the saving clarity presupposes the night
of the unconscious, and finds its climax in the blinding illumination of the
supraconscious. (P. Masson-Oursel : 'Indian Theories of Redemption', in *The
Mysteries*, p. 5.)

spiritual stirring all over the world, at least, all that part of the world which was then known and civilized. This is not the place to deal with the Mystery religions in any detail, but we must glance at some of them in order to see the way in which they formed some of the many streams which prepared the way for Christ and for the teaching of the Catholic Church.

The most typically Greek of all the ancient Mysteries were those of Eleusis, which were regarded as the archetype of them all, though possibly not the oldest. The Eleusinian cult was based on the myth of Demeter and Persephone, her daughter. The oldest document relating to this myth is the beautiful Homeric *Hymn to Demeter*, probably dating from the 7th century B.C. It appears to have been written to explain the origin of these Mysteries. The fact that in this hymn there is no mention either of Athens or the Athenians, who later played so conspicuous a part in the Mysteries, points to an early date for its composition, to the time when Eleusis was still a petty independent state, and before the great processions between Athens and Eleusis took place. [2] Though this myth has much in common with the oriental myths of Aphrodite and Adonis, Cybele and Attis, as well as the Egyptian myth of Isis and Osiris, the Greek version is unique in mythology for, whereas in the other myths the goddesses always mourn either a husband or a brother, in this Greek myth we find the purer and tenderer form of a mother mourning for her lost daughter. Demeter and Persephone were joined together in a great love, and though Persephone, or Kore, passes as the daughter of Demeter she often gives the impression of being her double. They were both corn goddesses, and are portrayed in art with wreaths of corn on their heads and holding stalks of corn in their hands.

There are many references and allusions to this myth in various authors, who give somewhat different versions. Briefly it is this. Kore-Persephone was a virgin-goddess of exceptional beauty who was kept safe by her mother Demeter on the island of Sicily. However, Pluto, king of the underworld,

[2] J.G. Frazer, *The Golden Bough* (abridged), p. 393.

set his heart upon having her as his wife, and as he could not obtain the consent of Demeter to this union he determined to obtain her by force.   While Persephone was playing in the meadow with her maidens she saw a flower of wondrous size and beauty and stooped down with delight to pick it.   At that moment the earth opened and Pluto appeared in his chariot, and in spite of Persephone's struggles carried her down to the underworld.   Demeter came hurrying along to look for her child and when she could not find her lit two torches at the fires of Aitna and wandered sorrowing over land and sea, her golden tresses veiled by a dark mantle.   At last the Sun, who had seen everything, told her what had happened, whereupon Demeter was furious with Zeus and the other gods for allowing such a thing.   Finally in her wanderings she came to Eleusis, where she took the form of an old woman and sat down sadly by the well of Parthenion.   Here the king's daughters found her when they came to draw water, and treated her kindly. One of them even persuaded her to smile by her jesting, a point which probably explains the fact that jesting and raillery formed a part of the Eleusinian Mysteries.   The girls then took Demeter to their home, where after a time she disclosed her identity, and demanded that a temple should be built in her honour.   When this temple was completed she hid herself in the sanctuary, far away from all the other gods, and mourned her lost daughter.   Then, and only then, did she bring about a terrible drought which lasted for a year.   All would have perished had not Zeus intervened and come to an understanding with Demeter whereby Persephone, though remaining Pluto's wife, should spend a part of each year with her mother.   With delight Persephone returned to Demeter, and Demeter in her joy made the corn to sprout in the fields and filled the earth with leaf and blossom.   Then she showed this lovely sight to the princes of Eleusis, and revealed her rites and mysteries.

The whole *Hymn to Demeter* leads up to this transformation scene, when the bare Eleusinian plain was suddenly transformed into a vast sheet of golden corn.   The revelation of the Mysteries is the grand climax.   In the poem we are given not only a general account of the foundation of the Mysteries, but also an explanation of the particular rites which are believed to have formed part of these Mysteries, such as the fast of the initiates, the torchlight procession, the all-night vigil, the jesting, and the communion with the divinity in a draught of barley water taken from a chalice. [3]

Who was Persephone?   There have been various theories. What death in nature is here portrayed, and what does the marriage with the King of the Underworld signify?   Possibly the most convincing suggestion is that the rape of Persephone is connected with the annual disappearance of vegetation. Whereas, however, in the other myths fertility disappeared from the earth when the goddess went to the underworld, this is not the case here, for only when the temple at Eleusis has been built in her honour does Demeter bring about the terrible drought.   If then Persephone is thought to personify grain, as has been suggested, her disappearance has nothing to do with the disappearance of fertility, for the drought only came later. Persephone's descent into the underworld *preceded* the raising of grain, for only after she was wedded to Pluto was there seed-time and harvest.

In this myth, then, we find an intuition which, however strange it may seem to us now, was entirely natural to primitive peoples— so natural that it almost seems as if 'existence itself had spoken to them' [4].   This intuition revealed to them that without death there could be no generation and no fertility: the growth of grain was particularly associated with death.   In the Biblical account itself procreation, birth and agriculture all appear after death had been decreed for mankind, that is, *outside Paradise*.   Amongst certain primitive peoples even to this day there is a tradition, which is regularly enacted in their cult festivals, that a mythical woman had to die in order that grain might spring from her limbs.   Only by initiation into her death can man receive power, and life be renewed.   Man receives fertility from the hands of death, and

---

[3] Ibid., p. 395.
[4] W. F. Otto, 'The Meaning of the Eleusinian Mysteries', in *The Mysteries*, p. 20.

to the Queen of the dead he must appeal. This is the core of the Demeter myth, for here, in Eleusis, Persephone was returned to her mother, and together they created agriculture. Here we see the worship of forces originating in the earth and returning to it. The fact that Persephone's husband was Pluto suggests the wealth of grain the earth provides year by year for the sustenance of man. The Eleusinian cult was thus devoted to 'one of the primordial forms of the soul's abysses, to a form suggesting the darkness before birth as well as the darkness after death' [5], to Mother Earth as represented by Demeter and her daughter Persephone.

This cult of the great Earth Mother was a *family* cult, attached to a particular place. The supreme initiations could only be received in the sacred bay itself at the hands of the representatives of the old priestly families of Eleusis. In all these primordial cults the great mysteries of life— birth, death and rebirth— rising from and returning to the darkness of the earth— are shrouded in darkness. They were related in some way to the moon, since they were enacted in the night, though sun worship replaced that of the moon in the later stages of the Eleusinian Mysteries. From various sources it can be gathered that in mid-September, when the quotas of grain arrived in Athens, a small sacrifice was made and then the Great Mysteries took place. After their completion the pilgrims apparently left Eleusis and went back to go on with the planting on their own lands, so here there was still something of the ageold idea of the primitive fertility cults, which were regarded as necessary in order to ensure a good harvest and the welfare of man and beast. The procession along the 'sacred road' leading from Athens to Eleusis— a distance of nearly fourteen miles— must have been a very popular one, for according to Herodotus 'three myriads' took part in it, and the dust they raised could be seen far and wide. A few days before this procession took place the cry had gone out 'To the sea, O mystai!', and the *mystai* had cleansed themselves from all stain in the vast sea. This ceremony was full of

[5] C. Kerenyi, 'The Mysteries of the Kabeiroi' in *The Mysteries*, p. 33.

symbolism, for here what was meant was not the sea that is used for navigation, but the primeval sea which was before the gods. Plunging into the sea those who took part in these Mysteries probably sought purification, for all the elements were regarded as having a purifying effect. Servius, commenting on Virgil's *Georgics* (II, 388), which dealt with the Mysteries, said, 'All purifications are effected by water or fire or air.' Yet it may also have signified a descent into the abyss of the unconscious, and a consequent 're-birth' or 're-creation'.

The great procession ended in a torchlight dance, a *lampadephoria*. The very stars of heaven were thought to join in this dance, and the waves, in which the lights were reflected, accompanied it, while Euripides states that even the moon herself joined in. The theological or mythical basis of this torchlight dance was probably that it represented Demeter carrying torches as she journeyed through the world seeking her missing daughter, though this is by no means certain.

These Mysteries, which rose up so overwhelmingly out of the depths of Greek life, were a heritage from a world into which the Greeks entered: they were the final outgrowths of pre-Aryan Great Mother religions. Though they were transfigured by the Greek spirit, they were in essence *pre-Greek*. In them Hellenistic religious experience was, as it were, *mysterized*, a process which went on developing during the early Christian era. The whole atmosphere of the first century A.D. was one of 'mystery'. In the second century there was a change, and a solar pantheism entered into the countless forms of mystery religions, even into the most famous of them all which we have been considering. The real background of these religions were the primordial Great Mother religions which centred round the goddesses and their consorts. They were fertility cults, for the Great Mother was the embodiment of the ever-resurgent face of nature. Yet behind these fertility cults, with their emphasis on the annual death and revival of nature, those who enacted them saw something else. The symbols of the power and processes of nature were only one part of them: the other part went out into the 'beyond', into that other world which transcended death. Very early the Mystery religions became associated with hopes of an after life, and thus they were a symbol for the whole mystery of life.

The Mysteries were a religion of feeling rather than of intellect. The central and enduring element in them was the performance of certain rites. *Mysteria* was the name given to certain festivals in Athens: the original pagan Greek word had nothing to do with the eastern and western idea of 'mysticism'. It was, rather, a festival, a fixed event on the calendar, and the term *mysteria* related to the time filled by the rites themselves, that time when those who took part in them came out of profane time into the 'Sacred Great Time'. In Athens, though often the deities were not specifically mentioned, it was apparently taken for granted that Demeter and Persephone were the goddesses of these Greek festivals. In one sense these rites were probably not 'secret' at all, for what took place in them must have been known to those who lived in the vicinity, but there was a 'sacred open secret'— something that could not be uttered or expressed. Therefore in the deepest sense there was in them a true 'mystery', something entirely secret because it was mysterious. It was not by accident that these rites took place at night:

> The Mysteries were so essentially nocturnal that in them every aspect of the night was experienced, even that power residing solely in the night, the power to engender light as it were, to help it to come forth. They were not merely a nocturnal festival, they actually— or at least it seems so— solemnized the feeling of being shut in by the night, culminating in a sudden great radiance. [6]

The preparations were made at the full moon, but the moon was already on the wane when the mystai plunged into the sea for their purifying bath, and this, too, was surely not by accident.

Professor Kerenyi has illustrated the difference between the two aspects of the 'secret' by comparing it with two different concepts of 'life' itself: the 'existential' and the purely

[6] Ibid., pp. 39, 40.

'rational'.   He has shown that on the first plane when we are
deeply moved by our actions or sufferings we can find no
words with which to express what we feel at all adequately.
On the second plane, however, on the 'rational' one, biological
currents can be quite clearly and adequately and unemotion-
ally expressed.   It is actually the same *life* that is described in
biological terms, but it is not *me*, not my *real* life.   My *real* life,
my interior life, which is so vital and moving, cannot be
expressed in these terms, for it is inexpressible.   The *true*
mystery is something experienced and lived, the essential thing
about it is not that it is something *secret*, but that it is *mysterious*:
a mystery.   Only in the 'cult' can our own intimate personal
experience be raised towards the universal so that it still
remains *our own ineffable mystery* which, nevertheless, we have in
common with all men. [7]

What, after all, is myth?   The story of our original ancestors
handed down from age to age?   Yes.   But the past is only part
of the myth.   The true myth is bound up with the cult: the
'Mysteria'.   That which once was, or is thought to have
been, is also a living event, here and now.   The cult re-enacts
an archetypal event situated, indeed, in the past, but *in essence
eternal*.   The gods are at hand as they were at the beginning of
time; the supreme realities of the present, the creating and
suffering powers of the present moment, which also encompass
death itself, are in touch with the gods in that 'sacred time'
in which the Mysteries are enacted.   The Mysteries took the
initiates back to the very beginning of life.   The marriage
of Persephone and Hades or Pluto which was celebrated in the
Mysteries was a prototype of human marriage.   When in
ancient times a bride was given to her betrothed she was
covered as in death, and so were the mystai, though for men this
never held such depths of meaning as it had for that goddess
who surrendered herself to the god of the underworld.   By
mythological images the initiates were led back to the natural
roots of their being: they were brought into contact with the
world of their ancestors.   In Christianity the 'Mysteries'—

[7]Ibid., p. 37.

above all the Sacraments of the Church— were new and
powerful instruments by which men might be rooted in a wholly
different and a supernatural realm, but the symbolism remains
the same. 'Know ye not' says St. Paul, 'that when ye are
baptized into union with Christ ye are baptized into his
death?' (Rom. 6:3):

> Therefore we are buried with him by baptism into death:
> that, like as Christ was raised from the dead by the glory of
> the Father, even so we also should walk in newness of life. For
> if we have been planted together in the likeness of his death,
> we shall be also in the likeness of his resurrection (6:4-5).

Fundamentally all the veiling and mystery of the Mystery
cults was a means of attaining to a realm which lay beyond
all the trappings and actions and even the words of the cult.
They knew that without death there could be no life; without
dying no fertility. St. John tells us that when the Greeks came
and asked to see Jesus, the Lord exclaimed at once

> The hour is come that the Son of Man should be glorified.
> Verily, verily, I say unto you, Except a corn of wheat fall into
> the ground and die, it abideth alone: but if it die it bringeth
> forth much fruit (Jn. 12:23-4).

The Cross may, indeed, have been foolishness to the Greeks,
but the 'mystai' would at least have understood the meaning
of these words.

In these Eleusinian Mysteries various degrees of insight and
initiation were transmitted by ritual word and action. First,
as we have seen, the mystai were cleansed from all stain in the
great sea into which they plunged at the commencement of the
festival. In the cult they fasted and drank a sacred potion,
and then came some illumination. The supreme rite was
called *epopteia*. Having passed through the dark and terrifying
night at the crucial moment a most brilliant light shone forth,
and those who had passed through terror and darkness were
suddenly transformed, their darkness was turned to light, their
fear into joy. But how, and in what way? This we shall

probably never know with any certainty, for on this point which is of most interest to us we still have the least information. What actually, befell the initiates? A Homeric hymn declares 'Happy is he who has seen'. We can only conjecture as to what may have taken place. The Roman bishop Hippolytus said that at the climax of the Eleusinian Mysteries an ear of wheat was displayed. It is possible that thus the immense life-giving power of the Earth Mother was impressed upon the initiates. But surely this was a common sight. On the other hand, there appears to have been something miraculous about this ear of wheat. Was some kind of magic act performed? In the season when no grain grew an ear of wheat appeared, growing with miraculous suddenness. These plant miracles are to be found in the festivals of many primitive peoples. Thus the mystai would have been transported into the realm of miracle, into the presence of the great goddesses themselves. The Eleusinian *mystes* would have experienced the presence of his goddesses and entered into intimacy with them: he would have been received into another sphere— into the sphere of the gods— and thus have been transformed. In the great moment, the central moment of the Mysteries, Persephone was present for mankind. We must not belittle what took place in these Mysteries, for they were venerated by such men as Sophocles and Euripides.

Our most important and reliable record of that sacred night is that of Apollodorus of Athens, who tells us that at the moment Persephone was called a kind of bronze gong was struck. Similar gongs were struck at the death of the Spartan kings, and it was apparently an ageold ritual preserved both in Sparta and in Eleusis. The kingdom of the dead burst open! Persephone was summoned from the depths. Heracles declared that he had descended into the underworld and had seen everything. 'I have seen Kore' he said. On this point Dr. W. Otto has compared the Greek Mysteries, in their purest state, with some of the Oriental cult rites, such as the Chinese invocation of Confucius, in which the simplest settings and actions produce an effect on all present which is quite overpowering. At the crucial moment, when the sublime Spirit who has been summoned prepares to appear, the great drum begins to beat, slowly and solemnly at first, then more and more rapidly, and finally in a breath-taking rhythm. Even the most enlightened observer, he declares, can no longer doubt the presence of the supernatural. [8] In Eleusis there was probably even more. The initiates had been brought close to the goddesses by the preceding ritual, by fasting, by drinking a potion, and so on. A bond had been forged between them; they were taken up into the myth, and in that supreme moment the myth became a reality. What they experienced was *secret* because it was ineffable and inexpressible. They sought the highest they knew, they longed for union with the divine, and though their formulation of the divine truths was crude and inadequate, built on strange and mythical foundations, surely God did not withold from them, from His children who knew their spiritual need and turned their faces to the light, some measure of His divine presence.

What was actually enacted in these Mysteries and what befell the initiates we shall never know with any certainty, but Aristides, writing in the second century, says of them that 'of all divine things that exist among men, it is the most terrible and the most luminous'. He speaks of the ineffableness many had been privileged to behold. There are many such descriptions, and we must treat them with respect. On the other hand, we must draw a sharp line of distinction between them and 'the truth as it is in Christ'. At no stage in their history do the Mysteries bear comparison with Christianity. The God of the Christian is not an intellectual construction or an embodiment of yearnings, however sublime, such as that which grew out of the religious search of the Greeks. He is not the God of the learned, or even only of the mystics, but the God of the Old Testament, the Living God, who after long centuries of preparation revealed Himself in Christ Jesus, whom the prophets had foretold. The faith of the crucified and risen Lord brought a message of such absolute reality and truth that those who were able to hear that message knew that they

[8] W.F. Otto., *op. cit.*, p. 29.

had come into the true light of life and knowledge. The Mystery religions, like the ancient myths from which they sprang, were man's pathetic attempt to raise and purge himself by his own efforts, while in Christianity it is not man who raises himself, but God who descends and confers on man that divine power which brings him into union with God in Christ.

The *life* Christ brought us is something entirely new: it is 'eternal life'. The basic dogmas of Christianity are that man was originally the child of God, that he lost his supernatural kinship by sin and regained it by the Cross of Christ, and that hereafter man will see God face to face— the God who *is* Love. The study of comparative religion can only reveal more and more clearly the absolutely unique character of Christianity. Though almost everywhere and in all stages of religious development, as we have already seen, there is a 'nostalgia for Paradise', for a return to that time which was *in the beginning*, when men enjoyed familiar intercourse with the gods, in Christianity there is a new element. The Christian no longer seeks to return to that condition in which the first Adam walked in the Garden of Eden, for *in Christ*, in the 'Second Adam', he believes that God has given us something much greater: union with God in Christ, and this life 'in Christ' is not only a matter of the hereafter, though only then will it be enjoyed in its fulness, nor is it a life only attained to in ecstasies, but it is a life of union which begins here and now, in this life, in which our souls and bodies are nourished and transformed by the sacramental feeding upon the flesh and blood of Christ, the Son of God:

He that believeth on me hath everlasting life (Jn. 6:47).
Whoso eateth my flesh and drinketh my blood, hath *eternal life* (6:54).
He that eateth my flesh and drinketh my blood dwelleth in me and I in him (6:56).

The 'mysteries' of the Kingdom of Heaven are the 'secret revelation' of Jesus; they are hidden under the cloak of parables. It is the 'secret of the King', which may not be cast before swine. It is the very purpose of God throughout the ages which is now revealed and made known, manifested to the saints (Col. 1:26). St. Paul was convinced that he had been entrusted with the secret of the universe, that' God was in Christ reconciling all things to himself' (2 Cor. 5:19). And who, he cries, shall separate us from this love of God which is in Christ?

> I am persuaded that neither death, nor life, nor angels, nor principalities, nor powers, nor things present, nor things to come, nor height, nor depth, nor any other creature, shall be able to separate us from the love of God, which is in Christ Jesus our Lord (Rom. 8:38-9).

This was a conviction the Mystery religions could never bring. The Christian Mystery is, nevertheless, more mysterious than any other: ' It is the very mystery of God, reflected in the secret of conscience. Otherwise all is clarity... It is a mystery in broad daylight.' [9] It is the mystery of God Himself.

St. Paul, as he travelled through those regions in which the Mystery religions held such sway, must have known much about them, and when he spoke of the 'weak and beggarly elements of the world' he may well have been referring to Mother Earth, to Demeter and Pluto. He offered to the Christian converts to whom he wrote something widely different: 'The unsearchable riches of Christ'. His great and universal mystery, the secret hid in God throughout the ages, and now at last revealed to man in Christ, is for all: it is no longer bound up with any soil or nation, with either Jerusalem or Eleusis, but is for Jew and Gentile, bond and free, rich and poor. *All* are to be brought together in Christ Jesus. Nevertheless we must see in the great pagan Mysteries which for seven centuries held sway in the Mediterranean world, right through into the Christian era, one of the rivers which were prepared to flow into the Church of Christ. These typically Greek Mysteries of Eleusis which we have considered may possibly be

---

[9] J. de Menasce, O.P., 'The Mysteries and the Religion of Iran' in *The Mysteries*, p. 140.

regarded as the highest and most developed form of the cult of
the gods which goes back into pre-history and which extended
far beyond the Greek world.   The Eleusinian initiates lived
in the intimacy of their goddesses and experienced their
presence.   They did not merely look on, but were actually
transformed in some measure to newness of life.   Here we find
the religious instinct of 'rebirth', though not in the sense
connected with this word in Eastern thought.   In a sense
they sought to return to the condition before the Fall, when men
walked with the gods in a beautiful intimacy, the time when
men still lived in Paradise, or that 'Golden Age' to which the
heart of man for ever turns with nostalgic longing.   As we
reflect on these Eleusinian Mysteries we shall find much in
them that is true and beautiful, and which prepared a vehicle
for the expression of the religion of Christ, the Incarnate Lord—
an expression without which the Church would have been less
able to show forth the fulness of Christ, and in Him the fulfilment of God's purpose of bringing men in the wholeness of
their mind and body, their imaginations, and all the God-given
instincts of their nature, into union with Himself.   Though we
may not postulate a direct influence of these Mysteries on the
development of the fundamental doctrines and formulations
of the Faith, certain aspects which had been developed in
them were made use of by the early Church for the more
perfect expression of her worship.

At Athens, barely fourteen miles from the great centre of the
Mysteries at Eleusis, whose temple had been built in the
mid-6th century B.C., St. Paul found an altar with the inscription 'TO THE UNKNOWN GOD', and declared that he
could bring them the knowledge of that God whom they
ignorantly worshipped.   The inscription bore witness both to
the ignorance of and also to the longing for, that ' unknown
God ', and therefore the soil here was ready to receive the
blessed and life-giving seed of eternal life and the knowledge of
the true God.   St. Paul's acquaintance with the Mysteries
cannot be seriously questioned.   When, in writing to the
Corinthians he says, 'We speak wisdom among them that are
perfect' (1 Cor. 2:6) he uses the word *teleioi*, the technical

term in the pagan Greek Mysteries for those who had received the highest grade of initiation. The very terms for the various stages of the mystical life in Christian mystical theology— purgation, illumination and union— were probably derived in the first place from those used in the ancient Greek Mystery cults.

The extent of the influence of the Greek Mysteries on the development of early Christianity has been a subject of wide-spread interest during the past century. Various theories have been put forward as to the extent of this influence, and though the research undertaken with a view to clarifying this question has led to a knowledge of the Mysteries which far exceeds that of earlier times, much is still far from clear. In the course of their study scholars have discovered much in these religions of late antiquity which was wholly lost to the Middle Ages. The latest theories are characterized by scrupulously scientific research, and are therefore probably far more accurate than the earlier ideas on the subject. Modern scholars distinguish very carefully between real *dependence*, and the dependence of adaptation. The Hellenistic Mysteries did not actually achieve their full development until the beginning of the 2nd century A.D., and therefore when St. Paul or the Church Fathers of the earlier centuries, who gave form to the Christian *cult*, borrowed words, images and gestures from these 'mysteries', they did so as possessors of their own very distinctive and incomparable religious tradition. What they borrowed was not the *substance* of their Faith and teaching, but simply the contemporary dress in which to express it, since this was the form in which it could best be understood by the people of their day. Clement of Alexandria, the Christian Platonist of the late 2nd century put this quite clearly when he said:

I shall explain the mysteries of the Logos in images that are known to you (Protrepticus XII. 119.1).

Recently there has been a tendency to stress the essential differences between the two religions. In fact, scholars may have gone too far in this direction in declaring that they are

utterly incompatible, for, however distinctive every religious
tradition may be, there is, nevertheless, an underlying element
in the human search for divine truths which must be present in
every form of religion: man's thirst for God is part of his very
being.   There is a 'nostalgia for Paradise' in every culture,
a sense of incompleteness and need which surely arises *either*
from the fact of a 'lost Paradise', a 'nostalgia' in the collective
subconscious of our race for a condition which it once enjoyed
but which it has now lost, *or* which is simply the response of the
depths of the soul of man to the magnetic, yearning love of
God— of the Logos, the Second Person of the Blessed Trinity,
the Word made Flesh— for union with whom we were created.
St. John expressed it in familiar words: 'We love him because
he first loved us ' (1 Jn. 4: 19).   Men yearn for union with
God, for that state of perfection when we shall be like
him, 'for we shall see him as he is', because He first draws
us to himself.   That the form of the response should be so
infinitely rich and varied only points to the depths and heights
of the mystery of our life and being.   Again, it is surely possible
that many saintly souls who have no knowledge of Christianity
are partakers of the uncovenanted mercies of God: without
actual knowledge of the Jesus of history, without incorporation
into Him by baptism, it is still possible that they may come to
very real union with Christ, for did He not himself say:

> They shall come from the east, and from the west, and from
> the north and from the south, and shall sit down in the
> kingdom of God (St. Luke 13:29).

The Church was not a ready-made structure.   It is a continuous incarnation of God, and its history is the embodiment
of revelation.   In the lovely words of Father Hugo Rahner
' The soul of this body which we call the Church is of heaven—
but its blood is of the Greeks and its language is of Rome. ' [10]
There were three ways in which the pagan Mysteries could
have influenced the early Church.   In the first place, since the

---

[10] Hugo Rahner, S.J., 'The Christian Mystery and the Pagan Mysteries'
in *The Mysteries*, p. 345.

Christian revelation is a revelation to man, who is a creature of flesh and spirit, the eternal truths which it revealed had of necessity to be expressed in terms which could be grasped by man, that is, in words and images and gestures. It had to make use of the ageold symbols that had been handed down through the centuries. Certain symbols and images in their basic form are present in every religion, for they are the archetypes of the human search for God. It is not possible to start from nothing, from a vacuum, and the Christian faith came into a world rich in religious history and in spiritual experience, which had impressed itself on humanity. In fact, as we have seen, these symbols and rites and images were part of that agelong process by which God prepared man for the Incarnation. The 'God-orientated' nature of man (Rahner) gave form to its experience of the divine in these symbols and words, for God can only speak to us by means of those ways which He Himself has given us of grasping in some measure the eternal mystery which lies at the heart of all. Christianity had of necessity to make use of those words and rites and symbols which were current in the world into which it went, otherwise its message could not have been understood. Secondly, there is also the possibility that the influence of the day penetrated into, and to some extent, influenced her teaching, though the truth of the Gospel once grasped could have allowed but little infiltration from the Mysteries. What influence there was would not have been on anything of importance, but on inessentials. Probably one of the most important and lasting effects of the thought of the time on Christianity was the influence on its baptismal teaching during the earlier centuries. The thought of purification, of washing, was so much to the fore at the time, with the idea of the newness of life which followed, that the Christian teachers were quite naturally led to stress the thought that baptism was *the* way of purification, of illumi- nation. Thus for two or three centuries St. Paul's doctrine of our *incorporation* into Christ, of baptism into union with Christ, was relegated, in some parts at least, to the background, though by the middle of the 4th century such saints as Cyril of Jerusalem and Ambrose of Milan re-emphasized the Pauline baptismal teaching. Thirdly, the contact between Christianity and the Mystery religions may have been part of the purpose of God, a purpose running through all ages, of preparing men for the coming of the Saviour, orientating them to this saving Mystery, for 'God left not himself without witness' (Acts 14:17). The Greeks, to whom the Mysteries meant so much, had at Athens an altar to 'the unknown God' (Acts 17:23). What more perfect preparation could there have been for the Gospel message— for the revelation to the beauty-loving Greeks of the life of the Incarnate Lord of whom the prophet wrote ' when we shall see him, there is no beauty that we should desire him' (Is. 53:2). It is small wonder that as this message spread through the Mediterranean world those whose hearts were prepared for its revelation were able to say in very truth that their eyes had seen 'the king in his beauty' (Is. 33:17).

CHAPTER XIV

SOME AFTER-LIFE CONCEPTIONS

A MONG THE GREEK Mystery cults there is one other we must consider, both on account of the after-life conceptions formulated in it, and also because of the influence it had on later Christian teaching through Plato and the Neo-Platonists. There were striking similarities between the Orphic and the Eleusinian Mysteries, for the centre of them both was the same: purification, fertility and rebirth. Both, in varying degrees, reached out to a luminous other-world.   Yet there is no possibility of proving that the Orphic cult, probably the older of the two, actually influenced the Eleusinian Mysteries. It would seem that both these Mysteries sprang spontaneously from the religious thought and feeling of their time.   While the Eleusinian Mysteries were the typical expression of purely Greek religious life the Orphic cults derived much from the Phrygian, Phoenician and Egyptian Mysteries which gave to the Mediterranean world the idea of destiny and a doctrine of 'being'.   The Punjab on the one side and Asia Minor on the other were the outermost points of the Persian Empire, and probably both received something from the religion of Iran.   In the Ionian corner of Asia Minor, though the world still consisted for them, as it had in days of old, of gods and men, there was no idea of a transcendent Being.   Neither was there any metaphysical or ethical distinction between men and the gods; the only thing that really separated them was that very ancient thought that the 'gods' alone enjoyed immortality— that immortality which is always one of the most continuous and important features of the idea of Paradise.   In the 7th century, however, a religious revolution, which reached even to the shrine of Apollo at Delphi, came to Greece with the coming of the god Dionysus from Thrace.   With it came something that was, in a sense, wholly 'un-Greek': 'wild ectasy, dark terror, the idea of guilt and atonement, condemnation and election'. [1]

This cult spread with amazing rapidity though Greece, Italy and Sicily during the 7th and 6th centuries before Christ, for it seemed to give the people something that the older state religions of Greece and Rome had failed to give: it satisfied elements in their being which had lain dormant, but which responded with fervour to the new religious teaching. By the middle of the 6th century the Orphic doctrines had influenced philosophical thought, and a spiritual development followed which cannot be overestimated. Pythagoras and the Pythagoreans in Southern Italy, as well as Pindar and the tragic poets in Greece, reveal their influence. Song began to take the place of the cult. These songs, which enjoyed immense popularity with Orphic believers, were 'narrative songs' about the gods. Finally they were brought together in twenty-four books which have been called the 'Orphic Bible', though this term is not entirely correct because these rhapsodies were never given dogmatic authority and were constantly undergoing change.

The Orphic Mysteries, in which some of the most essential expressions of the Dionisian cult are to be found, were named after the mythical figure of Orpheus, a singer who could tame all creatures by his song and who could gather round him wild animals and trees, besides moving stones and cliffs by the magic of his music. Though by the beginning of the sixth century the story of Orpheus was definitely a myth, Plato, our most reliable authority on Orphism, saw him primarily as a man. Scholars are still divided as to his identity. Some think he was the creation of a cult group (O. Kern), while others consider that he was an early religious figure elevated to the sphere of myth (Nilsson and Peterich). It has even been suggested by Eisler that the name really meant 'fisherman' ('Orpheus the Fisher' London, 1921). An ancient tradition has it that

---

[1] W. Wili, 'The Orphic Mysteries & the Greek Spirit' in *The Mysteries*, Eranos Yearbook, II, p. 66.

Orpheus not only introduced the Mysteries but also created a theology of them.   The most important elements in the legend of Orpheus, whoever he was, are sacred songs, the idea of the other world, the ennobling of men by song and transcendence by the Mysteries and by the suffering of their founder, for Orpheus was rent by the wild women of Thrace.   According to him water was the beginning of everything.   From this water mud was formed, and from this mud an animal was produced: a dragon with the head of a lion and of a bull, and in between the face of a god.   It was called Heracles and Cronos. Heracles gave birth to an enormous egg, which through the power of its father got bigger and bigger and at last burst into two through friction.   The top was heaven and the bottom was the earth.   A biform god also came forth whose name was Phanes.

Dr. Walter Wili has tried to reconstruct the story of the threefold Dionysus in the form in which it may have been read by the aged Plato. [2]   Briefly summarized it is this.

In the beginning time created a silver egg, and out of the egg burst Phanes-Dionysus. His name shows that the root idea here is that of light.   Later the Orphics were not sure whether to interpret that as 'the Glittering One' or as 'the bringer of light'.   Clearly, in any case, he was a god of light.   He was also the first god to appear, and being bisexual he bore within him the seeds of all gods and men; he was, in fact, creator of all things in heaven and on earth, the sun and the stars, and the dwelling-place of the gods.   This god acquired various names, among them that of Eros. He bore within him infinite time and Eros, the all-creating.   In the 'holy legends' Phanes first created his daughter Nyx, night.   Zeus, the great-grandson of Phanes, could only gain dominion over the world by devouring Phanes, and thus the world of Zeus was a rebirth, enriched by the action of Zeus.   This devouring, however, did not imply any barbaric thinking.

Though Zeus was the most forceful of the Orphic gods their favourite god was the second Dionysus— Dionysus-Zagreus—

[2] Ibid., p. 71 ff.

whom Zeus begat upon his daughter Persephone.   Since he
was the son of Persephone, the Queen of the Underworld, he
was obviously a ruler of the dead, but while he was yet a child
Zeus also gave him rule over this world, as a symbol of which
the child Dionysus played with the apples in the Hesperides.
This roused the envy of the Titans, who tore him to pieces and
devoured him. In his rage at this brutal act Zeus destroyed the
Titans and burned them.   From their ashes, according to this
myth, the human race arose, and thus, though men were by
nature Titanic, having inherited the evil nature of the Titans,
they had nevertheless a spark of the divine as well, since before
their death the Titans had eaten the boy Dionysus.   This
conception of the Titanic nature has been called the 'Orphic
original sin'.   The Orphic cults were part of a contemporary
movement in the spirit of man in which there was a conception
of sin and atonement, stain and purification.   This may,
actually, be considered one of the most far-reaching conceptions
of the Greeks.   It taught that man must redeem himself by
fleeing from his Titanic nature and thus saving the Dionysian
side of him: the divine soul must strive to return to its source.
The outcome of this idea was that the body was thought to
imprison the soul, and the soul therefore had to seek flight into
the transcendent.   This flight from the world is, in essence, an
un-Greek conception.   The Orphics also believed in transmigration, and taught that the soul of man is eternal, the
individual soul having existed before its birth into this world,
and having immortality.   There were many rites of purification
and very strict rules of fasting, for besides abstaining from all
meat on account of their transmigration theories, the Orphics
were also forbidden to eat eggs, since the god Phanes was
born of an egg.   They were the first to conceive of an 'Isle of
the Blest' and of a Tartarus: the deep abyss beneath the ocean
which was the home of the Titans.   The first part of the Orphic
Mysteries dealt with man's sin and his purification, while
the second part dealt with redemption.   Much of the Orphic
teaching has been transmitted to us through Plato and his later
followers, such as Plotinus and Proclus, as well as the great
Alexandrian Christian Platonists of the 3rd century A.D.—

Clement of Alexandria and Origen.   This teaching is especially interesting because of its influence on the Church's doctrine of purgatory and the state of the faithful departed.

The trend towards a universal religion in pre-Christian times is first found among the Orphics.   They had no special places, no holy city which must be visited by those who sought redemption.   Their rites were performed in scattered 'sacred' houses, and they possessed no cult temple hallowed by tradition. This may to some extent account for the rapid spread of Orphism, though it must not be regarded as its main cause. The Orphic priests went about preaching and were, in fact, the first itinerant preachers in Europe.   Beginning at the latest during the 7th century B.C., Orphism continued right through to the early Christian period, while its literature lasted to the very end of pagan times.   Its doctrine and mysteries revolved around the concept of *immortality*.   The very word 'orthodoxy' appears for the first time to come into use among them. [3] Their missionaries, wandering from city to city, were convinced that they alone preached the right and true doctrines, and that the Mysteries they celebrated were in accordance with their orthodox teaching.   It is perhaps not surprising that the Christians of late antiquity should have compared Orpheus with Christ himself.   In the *Hymn to Demeter* we find the words:

> Happy is he among men upon earth who has seen these mysteries; but he who is uninitiate and who has no part in them, never has lot of like good things once he is dead, down in the darkness and gloom (Hymn to Demeter. 480).

This hymn begins with what is possibly the first beatitude in the Western world, expressing faith in the liberation from a 'dead' life by means of a sacrament, a mystery, a cult rite performed by a priest.   The influence of the Orphic-Dionysian cult can be traced right through the Middle Ages up to the 13th century.   We find it in a 12th century hymn to the mystery of the Cross:

[3] P. Schmidt, 'The Ancient Mysteries and their Transformation' in *The Mysteries*, pp. 105-6.

> As of old the serpent brazen
> Unto Israel brought salvation
> Lest in Pharaoh's bonds they die,
> So his bride our Orpheus raises
> From the nether deep, and places
> In his royal seat on high (Tr. A.S.B. Glover).

Orphism preached retributive justice, it spoke of purification and atonement, and it took a particular view of the future life. It created judges of the dead by whom evildoers were relegated to 'hell'— a place of muck and torment— while the good were assigned to the 'Isle of the Blest'.   It no longer conceived of the after-life as a copy of life on this earth, but divided it between the good and the bad.   Plato, who shows unmistakable Orphic influence in his later writings, has an interesting passage on this point.   He says that at the time of Cronos, and down to the time of Zeus, judgement was given on the day men were to die, immediately *before* their death, and the consequence was that often wrong judgement was given and souls found their way to the wrong place.   The reason for this was that the judges, as well as those who were being judged, *had their clothes on,* so that many having evil souls, because they had fair bodies and were attired in goodly raiment, overawed the judges, who were also unable to see clearly because they, too, had their clothes on.   Thus their eyes and ears and their whole bodies interposed before their own souls as a veil.   What, he asks, is then to be done that just judgement may be given?   The only answer to the problem is that men must be entirely stripped before they are judged, that is, they must be judged after death. The judge, too, must be naked, that is, dead, so that he, with his naked soul, shall pierce into the other naked soul immediately after a man dies, and has left behind him all that is of earth, his friends and relatives and all his brave attire (Gorgias. p. 523 b-e).

Now this belief in immortality, which is so characteristic of Orphism, began in Thrace, in the primordial Dionysian cult. On this point Baron von Hügel, in his book on the 'Mystical Element in Religion' made an interesting observation.   He pointed out that this distinctive and valuable teaching on the immortality of the soul was derived by the self-knowledge gained in

> that wildly orgiastic upheaval, those dervish-like dances and ecstatic fits during the Dionysian night-celebrations on the Thracian mountain-sides. [4]

He showed that it had been possible to trace the way in which the experience gained in this crude and extraordinary way, as well as the reaction against it in the Orphic sect, filtered through to Pythagoras, Plato and the Neo-Platonists, and that from them arose the clear conception and precise terminology concerning ecstatic, enthusiastic states. Here the divinity and the eternity of the human soul were realized, as well as its 'punitive lapses' into the imprisonment in the body, and its need of purification throughout the earthly life, and also of liberation at death. From these apparently repulsive circumstances and psycho-physical phenomena, from quite unmoral attitudes and activities, from excesses of feeling and conception, were derived the assurance of the 'downright eternity and increateness of the soul'. [5] Here, too, the entire disconnectedness of soul and body was realized. It seems strange that these insights should have been attained under such circumstances until we consider a factor which psychology has brought to light.

Recent studies in morbid conditions of the mind have thrown a flood of light on the character and workings of the healthy mind, which is much more difficult to analyse precisely on account of the harmonious interaction of all its faculties. The laws of illness, it has been observed, are at bottom the same as those of health, but the exaggeration of various phenomena in the unhealthy condition have revealed certain fundamental aspects of man's nature more clearly than is possible under normal conditions. Therefore it is not really surprising that in the past man has come to know more about certain aspects

[4] F. von Hügel, *The Mystical Element in Religion*, Vol. 2, p. 182 (lst ed.)
[5] Ibid.

of his nature in times of abnormal excitation. Here we may call to mind the various 'techniques' employed in many primitive and exotic cultures in the world to-day by which the 'shamans' or mystics of these societies attain to mystical states which are regarded as a temporary return to the paradisal condition. [6] The doctrines resulting from the strange night-celebrations on the mountain-sides of Thrace only needed careful pruning and harmonizing to reveal a great body of truth.   They discovered the distinctions between mind and matter, between intuition and reasoning, and the great superiority of mind over matter.   From this they gained the assurance that mind and intuition must be more like the cause of all things, like the Creator, than other and inferior realities and activities.   They obtained knowledge of the fact that the standards of objective and infinite Beauty and Goodness and Truth are indestructible, and that man is conscious of being bound to these standards. Furthermore that it is just his realization of this his obligation that constitutes man's relative greatness, and brings him that sense of failure which must lie behind all the doctrines of the Fall of man.   The experiences of early ecstatics in their various techniques for attaining to the mystical state are still, apart from revelation, our most solid ground for belief in immortality, for if man's mind and soul suffer so deeply from a sense of the contingency and immutability of all things it must itself be, at least partly and potentially, outside this flux, this ebb and flow of earthly life, which it so vividly realizes as '*not* Permanence, *not* Rest, *not* true Life'. [7]   Therefore the Dionysian teaching, especially in its clearer Orphic expression and as it was eventually developed by Plato and his followers, must not be wholly rejected but only re-interpreted in the light of further spiritual experience, of which this was one of the earliest expressions and interpretations.

Here, for a moment, we must turn aside from the consideration of Orphism to think about this question of 'techniques' for the attainment of spiritual experience.   For many centuries techniques of various kinds have been used in most religious

[6] For a detailed study of this point see M. Eliade, *Myths, Dreams and Mysteries.*
[7] F. von Hügel, *op. cit.*, p. 193.

traditions, whether they are the rather crude techniques of the archaic cultures or the far more developed ones, such as those of the Yogi and the Buddhist mystics. In this Christianity is strangely at variance with the earlier traditions, though even here during the first centuries of our era we can see much the same conception in the lives of the Desert Fathers, who underwent extraordinary mortifications, and at times lived naked among the wild beasts in imitation of the nakedness of Adam in Paradise. Spiritual techniques are not part of the Judeo-Christian tradition, where their place is taken by the insistence on the need for the acceptance of the disciplines of life itself, with all its difficulties and pain, by the seeing of the hand of God in all things and by surrender to the divine will. The mystics of the Church never fail to insist on the absolute necessity of *suffering* as a means to the closer knowledge of God, but this suffering is never self-inflicted, never sought for its own sake, but something which must mark every life dedicated to Christ and to his Cross. Christ promised the kingdom of heaven to his followers, he taught that those who left all for his sake would find an ample reward both here and hereafter, but it would be 'with persecutions':

> Blessed are ye when men shall revile you, and persecute you, and shall say all manner of evil against you falsely for my sake. Rejoice and be exceeding glad: for great is your reward in heaven: for so persecuted they the prophets which were before you (St. Matt. 5:11-12).

A priest I was privileged to know many years ago, whose life had been marked by much suffering, never wearied of insisting that there was only one real tragedy in any life, and that was never to have known suffering. Here there is a deep truth, since for the Christian the times of suffering, whatever their cause or their nature, whether physical or spiritual, inevitably bring us out of the *normal* condition of life and set us apart in loneliness and pain, into that state in which it is possible to gain those richer and fuller insights which in many other religious traditions are reached in some measure by means of spiritual disciplines of a different kind.

Plato, that great thinker without whom there would possibly have been no European culture as we know it, was in his later life strongly influenced by Orphism. In his writings he distinguishes between two different forms of expression: *logos*, which means a faithful representation of reality, and *mythos*, which for him meant at first everything contrary to *logos*, but later everything that could not be apprehended or expressed by *logos*, and therefore embracing certain elements of *logos*. [8] In his early works Plato still saw the other world in un-Orphic terms and, as in archaic thought, as a reflection of this world. The *Gorgias*, however, shows the turning point in his thought and the birth of his real ideas is revealed, such as the judging of souls after death in their naked condition. He gives us five conceptions of the state after death.

1) The idea that each soul has a place prepared for it in exact accordance with its moral and spiritual dispositions here below: like dispositions seek like places. [9] The original, divinely intended places for all souls are good, and for this congenital place each soul has a 'resistible but ineradicable home-sickness', or, in other words, a 'nostalgia'.

2) Plato pictures the purification of the imperfect soul on the shore of a lake where the soul has to wait. To the shores of this Acherusian lake many souls go when they die, and after waiting an appointed time which for some is longer, for some shorter, they are sent back to be born as animals. Here the Orphic theory of transmigration appears. Yet Plato also says that those who have lived neither ill nor well are purified and go to a place of ultimate happiness, with no mention of reincarnation. Those, again, who have committed crimes are cast into Tartarus, the pains of which they are compelled to undergo for a year, at the end of which time they are borne to the Acherusian lake, except those who are irremediable and who remain for ever in Tartarus. Here is real teaching on a future purgatory which is not far from the conceptions of St. Catherine of Genoa.

---

[8] W. Wili, *op. cit.*, p. 87.

[9] 'The king of the universe contrived a general plan, by which a thing of a certain nature found a seat and place of a certain kind. But the formation of this nature he left to the wills of individuals' (LAWS, X. 904a-e).

3) In the *Phaedo* there is a passage which states that those who have lived very virtuously go to their 'pure home, which is above ', and dwell in the Isles of the Just. Rhadamanthus, the chief of the three nether-world judges, 'looks with admiration on the soul of some just one, who has lived in holiness and truth, and sends him, without any intervening suffering, "to the Isles of the Blest"! where all is perfect happiness and no one ever dies'. The beauty of this fancy attracted even deeply religious writers, such as Pindar, whose own conception of a future life was more developed. [10]

Then Plato adds some words which are very reminiscent of St. Paul:

> I consider how I shall present my soul whole and undefiled before the Judge in that day. [11]

4) The insistence on the necessity of being judged 'naked', to avoid all possibility of a wrong judgement.

5) He teaches that a soul makes a spontaneous choice after death of that place or condition to which the effect of her earthly willings and her self-formation have conformed her. The souls immediately on their arrival in the other world are required to go before Lachesis, one of the Three Fates, and Lachesis, the daughter of Necessity, says to them:

> Your destiny shall not be allotted to you, but you shall choose it for yourselves. Let him who draws the first lot be the first to choose a life which shall be his irrevocably... The responsibility lies with the chooser, Heaven is guiltless.

---

[10] H.J. Rose, *A Handbook of Greek Mythology*, p. 80. He quotes some of Pindar's words on this subject :
'There the breezes of Ocean breathe about the Islands of the Blessed, and flowers of golden hue blaze, some on land, upon fair trees, while others the water nurtures, with garlands whereof they entwine their hands and brows...'
'Before their city lie meadows ruddy with roses, shaded with balsam-trees, heavy-laden with golden corn. And some take their pleasure in horses and sports, some in draught-playing, some in the lyre, while all manner of wealth flowers fair among them. Also a sweet savour wafts over that lovely land, as they ever mingle every kind of incense in the far-shining fire upon the altars of the gods' (Olymp. II. 77(70) foll.).
[11] *Gorgias*, pp. 525c, e.

It was a truly wonderful sight, he assures us, to watch how each soul selected its life. Again, at the end of the first thousand years the good and the evil souls come to cast lots and choose their second life: and they may take any that they like. [12] The Destiny that accompanies each soul after its choice shows plainly that, though the choice itself is a free act, yet this choice is the necessary result of the soul's earthly volitions and self-development, and that the choice is not only an inevitable consequence of these, but also conditions its future choices. Plato outlines some of the choices made:

> The souls chose all manner of ways. The stupidest among them chose the life of a tyrant; Orpheus chose the life of a swan, since women had done him to death and he did not wish to be born of a woman again; Odysseus, finally, the shrewdest of all the Greeks, made the best choice, the life of a private man that had no cares. [13]

In the Orphic teaching there was an idea of a real purgation: a purifying away of the stains contracted by the soul in the course of its earthly life. Though it is not possible to ascertain whether Catherine of Genoa, whose 'Treatise on Purgatory' is a spiritual classic, had any knowledge of Platonic teaching, she shows a close affinity with Plato's thought, though probably quite unconsciously. Clearly her ideas are based on her own spiritual experience, for there is no 'purgatory' which does not begin in this world. For St. Catherine the 'places' in the other world are the different states and conditions of the soul. We are not plunged into *places* after our death, for the soul must not be thought of as moving in space unless it is held to a body. [14] St. Thomas Aquinas taught that each soul had a higher place assigned to it according as it approached more or less to God, whose seat is in Heaven. St. Catherine regarded the Fire of Hell, the Fire of Purgatory, and the Fire and Light

---

[12] *Phaedrus*, p. 149b.
[13] W. Wili, *op. cit.*, p. 89.
[14] 'Thou wast never a place, and yet we have receded from Thee; and we have drawn near to Thee, yet Thou art never a place.' St. Augustine.

of Heaven as most appropriate symbols of the various impressions produced by God's *identical* presence in each soul. In them all there are the two constant realities: the Spirit-God and the spirit-soul, in various stages of inter-relationship. Her picture of fire and heat is perfectly Christian and moral: fire represents the state of conflict and pain, while the sunlight is frequently with her a symbol of achieved peace and harmony. Clement of Alexandria taught that the 'fire of purgatory' is a rational, spiritual fire which penetrates the soul. He made no secret of the fact that his chief source for the formulation of his convictions on this point was the teaching of Plato. 'Men who are punished' he wrote, 'profit through their souls becoming better.' He also used the thought of *fire* which 'is the most severe form of correction to which the sinner can deliver himself. . . when all else has failed to turn him from sin, then "the fire consumes" '. [15] Yet this fire is a means of saving a soul from death; one of the many ways a loving Saviour uses to bring men to salvation. He pointed out that *fire* was one of the many means used by God in olden days, as in the Burning Bush and the Pillar of Fire. He thought of fire in two ways: one of which gave light, like the sun, and the other destroyed like earthly fire. The function of fire is to test, to purify, and to sanctify. The Fire of Purgatory was rather 'to destroy the foreign and base elements which have taken root in a man's soul, a painful operation which cannot be carried out without causing suffering'. [16] Fire, in the thought of the Early Church, was often applied to Baptism, and therefore we have the lesson of the Three Holy Children in the Baptismal rite for the Easter Vigil.

Origen thought that

each sinner himself lights the flame of his own fire, and is not thrown into fire that has been lit before that moment and that exists in front of him. . his conscience is agitated and pierced by its own pricks. [17]

[15] Paed. I. 61.
[16] Anrich, *Clemens & Origenes als Begründer der Lehre vom Fegfeuer*.
[17] Origen, *De Prin. II*, 10,4.

St. John Damascene (d. 750 A.D.) says quite definitely that Hell is not a material fire, but is very different from our ordinary fire, and that we scarcely know what it is. [18]　Among the Western Fathers St. Jerome saw the fire which is not quenched to be the sinner's conscience which tortures him, while St. Augustine, who in his later days came to believe in the possibility of a purgatory, thought of the purgatorial fire as the fire of the sufferings of this world.　Commenting on St. Paul's passage in 1 Corinthians 3:11-15, which is one of the scriptural texts on which the idea of purgatory is based, he wrote:

> Souls which renounce the wood, hay, straw, built upon that foundation, not without pain indeed (since they have loved these things with a carnal affection), but with faith in the foundation, a faith operative through love.. arrive at salvation, through a certain fire of pain... Whether men suffer these things in this life only, or such like judgments follow even after this life— in either case, this interpretation of that text is not discordant with the truth.

Man shall be saved as by fire, because the loss of the things that he loves burns him; therefore it is not incredible that 'some such things take place even after this life... that some of the faithful are saved by a certain purgatorial fire, more quickly or more slowly, according as they have more or less loved perishable things'. [19]

For St. Catherine of Genoa there was One God, who is the Fire of Pain and the Light of Joy to souls according to whether they resist Him or surrender to Him, here and hereafter. Her teaching is less definite than that of Plato.　Man's spiritual personality was held by her to survive death and to retain its identity, or a consciousness equivalent to it, and she thought that the deepest experiences of that personality during its earthly life were then re-experienced in a heightened form.

Therefore the great pictures she gives of the soul's experience after death really express that soul's desires and requirements

---

[18] *De Fide Orthod.*, cap. ult.
[19] *De Octo Dulcit*, Quaest. 12-13.

here, in this life, and would remain profoundly true even if there were no after-life. Her own spiritual experiences were projected into the future, and though she, possibly unwittingly, reproduced much of Plato's later teaching, she omitted his theories of transmigration and other non-Christian ideas, regarding everything as penetrated by God's presence, grace and love, and conditioned by our own emotional and intellectual attitude. Of that 'plunge' into Purgatory which Cardinal Newman brought out so impressively in his 'Dream of Gerontius ', she says:

> Once and once only, do the souls (that are still liable to, and capable of purgation) perceive the cause of (their) Purgatory that they bear within themselves— namely in passing out of this life: then, but never again after that: otherwise self would come in. [20]

This momentary experience is at once followed by a unique momentary act— a perfectly free, full act on the part of the experiencing soul, which Catherine describes in every kind of mood and from a great variety of viewpoints.

> The soul thus seeing (its own imperfection) and that it cannot, because of the impediment (of this imperfection) attain to its end, which is God; and that the impediment cannot be removed from it, except by means of Purgatory, swiftly and of its own accord casts itself into it. [21]

The soul, in its ascent to God, is absolutely impeded in its swift movement and brought to a dead stop as by something hard on its own surface which makes a barrier between itself and God. This causes the soul the most intense suffering, and finding one way open to it of removing this terrible barrier which prevents the attainment of that union with God which is its sole desire, it plunges into the ocean of fire where alone the hard obstacle may be dissolved.

[20] *Vita*, pp. 173a-173b-33b.
[21] Ibid., p. 175b.

If the soul could find another Purgatory above the actual one, it would, so as more rapidly to remove from itself so important an impediment, instantly cast itself into it, because of the impetuosity of that love which exists between God and the soul and tends to conform the soul to God. [22]

She reveals her sense of the *Holiness* of God:

I see the divine essence to be of such purity, that the soul which should have within it the least mote of imperfection would rather cast itself into a thousand hells, than find itself with that imperfection in the presence of God. [23]

The soul, realizing that Purgatory was ordained for the very purpose of purging away its stains, gladly casts itself into it, and feels the great compassion of God who allows her to do so. This initial act, this *plunge* into Purgatory, is freely chosen, but in her teaching it is followed by a *continuous* state: the will that had at that one moment chosen Purgatory, must abide, however painfully, by its decision.

The souls that are in Purgatory are incapable of choosing otherwise than to be in that place, nor can they turn their regard towards themselves, and say: "I have committed such and such sins, for which I deserve to tarry here"; nor can they say "Would that I had not done them, that now I might go to Paradise"; nor yet say "That soul is going out before me"   ....They are so completely satisfied that He should be doing all that pleases Him, and in the way it pleases Him, that they are incapable of thinking of themselves.

They are, in fact, incapable of even seeing themselves directly, for

These souls in Purgatory think much more of the opposition which they discover in themselves to the will of God

[22] Ibid., p. 177b.
[23] Ibid., p. 175b.

than they do of their own sufferings. To do otherwise would
be to let self come in:

> These souls do not see anything, even themselves in
> themselves, or by means of themselves, but they (only) see
> themselves in God. [24]

Since they have their wills thus fully united with the divine
will and with God's purifying action, Catherine concludes:

> I do not believe it would be possible to find any joy
> comparable to that of a soul in Purgatory, (despite the pain
> of the purgation) except the joy of the Blessed in Paradise.

There is in the soul an instinct which draws it to God, its
ultimate end, and since it finds itself as yet unable to attain
to its fulfilment

> an extreme fire springs up from thence (within it) a fire
> similar to that of Hell. [25]

On the other hand Catherine also conceives of the soul in
movement downwards 'from its own surface to its own centre',
a centre where resides its Peace, God Himself.

> When a soul approaches more and more to that state of
> original purity and innocence in which it was created, the
> instinct of God, bringing happiness in its train, reveals itself
> and increases on and on, with such an impetuousness of fire
> that any obstacle seems intolerable. [26]

In the more self-consistent form of her teaching, however,
the Fire, God, is always present, and the impediment simply
renders this fire painful. This is in accordance with the
teaching of St. John of the Cross, when he shows that the
divine light, shining on the impure soul, is like the light of the

[24] Ibid., pp. 169c, 170a-182b.
[25] Ibid., p. 172b.
[26] Ibid., p. 172a.

sun shining on diseased eyes and causing them intense pain, and speaks of the effect of the 'Living Flame of Love' as it dries up and enkindles the soul.

Now, as the souls in Purgatory, after that first blinding vision and the plunge into Purgatory, no longer see their sins, but feel in themselves a dull, dead remainder of opposition and imperfection, neither do they see God clearly till quite the end of their sufferings. At the moment of death they had seen God and their sins with blinding clarity— a clarity which brought piercing pain and the swift plunge into the purging ocean. Then came a period of comparative dulness and dimness, when in their subconscious being they felt, rather than saw, both God and their sins. At first the latter were more prominent than the former, but all in a state of flux and transformation. Gradually the sense of their sins faded out and the love of God became clearer, and with it came light and life, joy and harmony, peace and contentment. And this growing sight of God was blissful beyond words, for

> every little glimpse that can be gained of God exceeds every pain and every joy that man can conceive without it. [27]

Gradually the covering of the soul is burned away in Purgatory, and the sin which caused it is consumed in the loving fire of God:

> Sin is the covering of the soul; and in Purgatory this covering is gradually consumed by the fire; and the more it is consumed, the more does the soul correspond and discover itself to the divine ray. [28]

When at last the soul is wholly purified it abides in God. Here God and the Fire are one and the same. The soul *remains* in the Fire, and the Fire remains where it was, God. The only difference is that the foreign substance, the

---

[27] Ibid., p. 182b.
[28] Ibid., p. 170c.

impediment, has been burnt out, and that Fire which at first caused it so much pain, now delights it.

> The soul, thus purified, abides entirely in God; its being is God. [29]

The teaching applied by St. Catherine to Purgatory and the after-life is applied by St. John of the Cross to the spiritual life here and now. The fire is that which burns out the imperfections of the soul in the 'dark night of loving fire', and when these impediments and stains are thus burned away the soul attains to true union with God, to the Spiritual Marriage. All St. Catherine's teaching on Purgatory may very fruitfully be applied to this life on earth, and Baron von Hügel, who spent many years of his life in the study of her life and doctrine, prayed that he might have all his purgatory, every drop of it, in this world, and then, at his death, the vision of Christ, of God, with all joy, all purity, all peace.

[29] Ibid., p. 178b.

CHAPTER XV

NIRVANA

THE FAR EASTERN cultures, so esoteric and so difficult for our Western minds to understand, present us with a concept of a 'Fall' and a 'Paradise', or ultimate beatitude, which differs widely both from those of the primitive cultures and from Judeo-Christian thought. At the outset I feel I must say that in speaking, as it were, of alien cultures, and touching, however lightly, on these questions, I speak as from 'outside' and not from 'within' those traditions, and that where I may misrepresent any aspect of them, or draw any unwarranted conclusions, I must implore the leniency of those who see more clearly into those religious approaches.

There are certain principles which are found in all the 'high' religions of the world. These include belief in the reality of the Holy and Transcendent, that which Plato spoke of as the 'reality of all realities'. While this reality is transcendent— the 'wholly-other'— it is also immanent in all human hearts. Christian mystics have spoken of this as the 'apex' or 'ground' of the soul. This transcendent and immanent Reality is man's highest good. In Christ, as in much mystical experience even where he is not known, this Reality has revealed itself as love. The prophets of Israel experienced the grace and mercy of Yahweh. St. John has told us that 'God is love', not only 'loving' but Love itself, and the true source of all love. The way to God is also universally recognized to be the way of sacrifice, though the meaning applied to this concept varies widely. Possibly the most perfect summary of its meaning, in the highest sense, is that it is the complete surrender to God's love. This, simple as it may sound, is nevertheless completely beyond the capacity of fallen man; in fact, it may possibly be the realization of the impossibility of this self-surrender which has brought home to man the fact of his 'fallen' condition. The way of surrender must begin with renunciation and self-discipline just because man has lost the power of simple response to the divine approach, and with it the ability to accept the grace of God. This 'way to God' leads by prayer and contemplation to union with the Divine, it is mystical *union* even though it is only to a limited number that mystical *experience* is vouchsafed. The outcome of union with God is also everywhere seen of necessity to include the love of one's neighbour. 'No man has seen God at any time' says St. John, 'but he that abideth in love abideth in God, but if a man say 'I love God', and hateth his brother, he is a liar; for he that loveth not his brother whom he hath seen, how can he love God whom he hath not seen?' (1 Jn. 4:20). Jesus taught his followers to love their enemies, and to pray for those who despitefully used them, and this love for enemies was actually taught before Him by the Buddha, in whose religion it is carried to very great lengths amongst his most devoted followers.

Turning to the thought of the 'nostalgia for Paradise' in the Eastern cultures, we can probably do no better than to start with a consideration of the well-known idea of *Nirvana*. This thought of *Nirvana* is the leading idea in all Buddhism: it lies at the very heart of that religion and is the cause of its existence, yet it is extremely difficult to define what is meant by this concept. The Buddha, Prince Gautama, was born in 560 B.C. His people were rulers of a territory in north-east India. Gautama never questioned the validity of the ancient teaching of his people on re-incarnation, but sought a way out of the appalling misery and suffering that afflicted mankind.   He never claimed to have a 'revelation', but, in the words of a Buddhist Abbot of our day:

A flash of divine wisdom revealed to him the path to Nirvana— the Ultimate salvation and bliss, He realized that man's real self was a spirit, a spark of the divine Flame, a drop of the Boundless shining Ocean, imprisoned in the illusory world of Being...   Prince Gautama, full of compassion,

showed the way to his fellowmen so that the 'drop' could
slide back into the shining Ocean, and be free for ever from
the wheel of life. [1]

The Buddha accepted suffering as the lot of man, and taught
that only by complete renunciation of all desire can man attain
to release from suffering and to peace. Indian teaching in his
day, and I believe even now, thought of the law of 'Karma'
as imposing innumerable transmigrations and a constant return
to this world and hence to suffering. The ascetical and contemplative techniques in the East are therefore all directed to the
same end: to bring man release from the pain of existence in
time. One of the methods of thus 'burning up' time, is that
of 'returning to the past', of becoming conscious of one's past
lives. This is known throughout India, and was also known
to all the Buddha's contemporary contemplatives. The method
used is to cast off from a definite moment in time and retrace
time backwards, in order to arrive at the *origin*, the point when
existence first burst into the world and *time* began. By so
doing the contemplative joins that instant before *time* was, when
nothing had as yet been manifested. Thus to 're-live' one's
past lives is to see them in their true perspective and in so
doing to 'burn up' one's sins. The most important part of
this technique, however, is that one thus enters the 'timeless'—
the eternal present which preceded the 'Fall' into temporal
existence: the contemplative comes out into eternity, into the
'timeless' or the 'Great Sacred Time', and thereby transcends
the human condition by regaining the 'non-conditioned' state
which preceded existence with its constant cycle of re-incarna-
tions. [2]   The end at which Nirvana appears to aim is then this
negative one of being freed from perpetual transmigration.
    Etymologically 'Nirvana' means 'blowing out', 'cooling',
'deliverance',   'disappearing',   'refreshment',   'comfort',
'repose', 'serenity'. [3]   Strangely enough the West seems to
have been much more interested in trying to understand its

[1] P. Goullart, *The Monastery of Jade Mountain*, p. 55.
[2] M. Eliade, *Myths, Dreams & Mysteries*, pp. 49, 50.
[3] Hastings, *Encyclopaedia of Religion & Ethics*, art. Nirvana.

meaning than the East, for in the West we have sought to study the doctrine, while the Buddhists themselves seek rather to reach that blessed state than to define it. We look at the Buddhist teaching from the outside, while they from inside seek to reach Nirvana. Admittedly, its original meaning is a negative one. At the time of its inauguration, or discovery, men were tired of existence and this negative definition appealed to them, though to us it seems cold and barren. The old orthodox Buddhist teaching on the subject is very austere: deliverance is pure and simple annihilation. Yet from the very first this has raised questions and difficulties. When asked to state definitely whether deliverance really involved annihilation or not the Buddha Sakyamuni refused to give any definite answer. Even his early followers were dissatisfied. They had come to their master seeking for *immortality*, not extinction, and though his teaching was very clear on this subject they hoped they had misunderstood him. Many of them questioned him about Nirvana, but received no satisfactory reply. This was in a sense consistent with the Buddha's teaching, for he did not really believe that man had a soul— a doctrine which has led to very grave difficulties: he denied the survival even of saints. This doctrine of annihilation is not, however, a prominent one among the Buddhists, and was probably not a part of the founder's original purpose, but simply the result of his denial of the existence of a soul of man. There have, consequently, always been 'heretics': those who believed in personality, and, in spite of the severe teaching concerning it, Nirvana is looked upon with the deepest joy and hope. Possibly these feelings are due to mystical and religious experience which gives them a foundation which the orthodox creed refuses to supply. Actually a very important point in Buddhist teaching is that Nirvana is a place of happiness after death, and it is spoken of much as we speak of Paradise. For many centuries Christians believed in an 'earthly Paradise', and in many ways we still seek, however unconsciously, for a paradise in this world. Likewise many texts about Nirvana do not seem to imply deliverance from existence, but the bliss enjoyed by those who have freed themselves from all attachment to the things of this world. It may even be maintained that the monks seek only an *earthly Nirvana* without troubling themselves as to the future. The origin of the whole idea of Nirvana is most obscure, and though their sacred books insist that it is simply a concept— an idea of which nothing can be predicated— there can be no doubt that for thousands of Buddhists it has always meant an eternal repose.

We must be careful in our judgement of this doctrine of Nirvana as one of negation. Dr. R. Otto has recorded an interview he once had with a Buddhist monk on this question. Having had the details of the doctrine expounded with much care— an explanation which produced an impression of coldness and negative austerity— Dr. Otto asked to what this concept of Nirvana actually led. After a long pause the monk answered very softly 'Bliss unspeakable', and the way those words were said illustrated far more clearly than the words themselves all that lay behind them: all the inexpressible mystery and wonder which underlay this seemingly forbidding teaching.

At much the same time as the Buddha founded his religion, with its central idea of Nirvana, Confucianism and Taoism appeared in China. Confucianism was practical, while Taoism was philosophical. This philosophy, which has also gradually become a religion, has from the very first deeply affected Confucianism as well. It is now also very closely allied with Buddhism, though there is no fusion between the two religious outlooks. Fundamentally they are actually very different, for, whereas Buddhism is essentially pessimistic, Taoism is essentially optimistic. To the Buddhists the world is one of sorrow and suffering, sin and death, while to the Taoists, who believe in the process of Being, this world has many planes of existence which have all issued from the great Infinite Spirit. They argue that, since all creation is the work of Tao, the Eternal Spirit, it cannot be evil in its essence.

To make the world live and move the interplay of the Duality Principle, Yang and Ying, is a prerequisite— light and shadow, warmth and cold, sadness and joy; otherwise the Universe would become static and, if everyone was uniformly happy and content, all human progress would cease. The Taoists do not believe in a wheel of life to which all living beings are chained. Instead existence is visualized by them as a glorious, ever-ascending spiral of evolution. The whole universe, they teach, is a marvellous, vibrant Unity wherein everything, visible and invisible, pulses with life and consciousness. As consciousness develops through the experience of existence, its vessels— men and other sentient beings— are swept onwards and upwards by the mighty stream of the Eternal Tao to higher forms of expression and activity. Man does not die; he merely extends to new fields of consciousness. Nothing is lost and nothing is dead in this divine economy, and no being is left in unhappiness and suffering for ever by the Infinite Love. [4]

Taoism has many forms, and in its purest state, as practised by the Lungmen Taoists, it reminds one forcibly of the ideals that lay behind early Benedictine Monachism. For them the symbol of Paradise is the 'Abode of Haiwangunu', a retreat where both body and soul find joy and happiness, and which is the gate to the other, ultimate Heaven, which to the true Taoist is always just visible beyond the veil. The Tibetans call it Shambala. Sometimes the Taoists say they search for this paradise and find it almost by chance, sometimes they look for it and do not find it because they lack faith and courage. Sometimes, while finding it, they fail to recognize it, and it is gone. Those who do find it believe that here lies the portal to Nirvana.

Apparently there are still traces of Nestorian influence in some Chinese religious art, and one cannot help wondering how far Christian teachings have really influenced the development both of Taoist and Buddhist belief in the course of the centuries, for they show definite traces of this influence, just as the later forms of the Greek Mysteries received an influx from Christianity, and as they slowly died away became more and more susceptible to this influence. In the Far East there is one point in which they differ very much from the West, and that is that they do not look for gulfs between the various forms of religion,

---

[4] P. Goullart, *op. cit.*, pp. 56, 7.

but seek rather for similarities and unity, for they believe that all paths lead towards the same Ultimate Reality, and that though the Ultimate Truth is one it has an infinite number of different aspects, so that each form of religious faith reflects one facet of the Divine.   There is much of truth and beauty in this view, from which we in the West might learn something of great value, yet, on the other hand, it fails to bring any *assurance*, which is one of the blessings of the Christian faith.   Chinese missionaries have told of the spellbound interest with which a Living Buddha heard the story of the Prodigal Son:

> The forgiveness of that young man by his father I can understand, he said, but what of the burden of sin of previous lives, which binds us to the wheel of life?

For answer he was told that

> Our Lord Jesus Christ is the Door *out* from the past as well as the Entrance *into* a new and eternal life.

The Buddhist listened thoughtfully, and then accepted a copy of the New Testament in Tibetan, which he carefully hid in the folds of his red shawl. [5]   On another occasion these missionaries on their journeys found an old lady of seventy trembling with excitement at their approach, for she had heard that they were preaching the forgiveness of sins, a blessing in search of which she had spent many years in austerity and fasting.

> Tell me, she said, how sin can be wiped out.   I have kept all my vows, and made many pilgrimages, now tell me, what more I can do?
> You've done all this, Granny, they replied, but has any of your sin been forgiven?
> How can I know? she cried, How can I know? [6]

This was the answer they found everywhere among a people who practised the most rigid asceticism when they pressed them

[5] M. Cable & F. French, *Through Jade Gate*, 1927, p. 58.
[6] Ibid., p. 132.

to estimate the value of all their self-denial.   It is strangely impressive to find here this sense of sin and deep longing for forgiveness, this rigid self-discipline and together with it all a complete lack of assurance.   Some recent writers have express-ed the view that while Christianity is the religion for the West, Buddhism is the form required by the East, yet in view of such facts one cannot but feel very doubtful of the validity of such a conclusion.   What joy and relief the words of the Incarnate Lord would bring to many: 'Thy sins be forgiven thee.' Taoists do believe unofficially that their Divine Tao was incar-nate in Jesus Christ.   Surely in these Far Eastern religions we may see one of the great streams which prepared the way for the Incarnation, but which, unlike the contemporary religious revo-lution in the Mediterranean world, has failed to flow into the place prepared to receive it in the revelation of God in Christ. For us Paradise always lies in the East, and therefore we turn to the East in prayer.   We hear of devout Christians in the Middle Ages asking, as they approached death, to be placed so that they faced the East and Paradise.   In the Monastery of the Spirit's Retreat in China there is an altar piece representing the *Western* Paradise.   It is fitting that it should be so, for thus both from the West and from the East men turn towards that blessed spot where the Second Adam redeemed the human race. In one of the places in China to which pilgrimages are made there are many shrines, and the object of each pilgrim is to visit as many of these as possible.   These pilgrims are quite indefatigable, and the women come with their bandaged feet and tiny shoes, some of them no longer young, to climb those precipitous hills, a number of them even doing so on hands and knees in order to reach some apparently inaccessible rock-shrine. These shrines can often only be reached by crossing rickety wooden bridges which bear such inscriptions as 'The Heavenly Road' or 'The Short Cut to Paradise'. [7]

There is one order of Taoist monks who devote much of their time to the casting out of evil spirits.   Some years ago, apparently, the Chinese government asked them to investigate

[7] Ibid., p. 108.

the possibilities, and these young monks do the work with
the greatest devotion and at immense cost to themselves. Very
few of them live long, for the strain of the work drains all the
vitality out of them. We are brought back into the world in
which Jesus lived and moved, and can realize how tremendous
the impression must have been when with one word, calmly
and unmoved, he bade the evil spirits come out of a man, and
they came out. There was no strain here, no stress, but calm
assurance and authority. This power of casting out evil spirits
was bequeathed by Jesus to his disciples, but how often in these
days this is forgotten. We resort to psycho-therapy and drugs,
but seldom do we stir up the power which he promised us, and
call upon the Lord to cast out the evil spirits by his almighty
power. It is true that even his immediate followers had not
sufficient faith on many an occasion to take him at his word, but
that does not mean that the power is not there to be used.

However much we may feel that Christianity would bring
the answer to many of the deepest yearnings of the Eastern soul,
we must yet acknowledge the power and beauty of much in
these Eastern religions. Dr. Zimmer has pointed out that

> Christ and the Buddha have entered into the 'unconscious'
> of East and West because their historical lives had such power
> that they superimposed themselves on an already existing
> image in the unconscious, as variant and development. They
> could enter into pre-existing archetypal forms which they
> replaced and adapted to themselves. Christ was the perfect
> fulfilment of that ancient Oriental figure of the dying,
> sacrificed and resurrected god of the seasons, Buddha of the
> old Indian sun-god. They possessed such stature that only
> those venerable lofty forms could cloak and preserve them
> down the ages. Thus they were able to inspire the unconscious
> of men far removed from them in time and space and touch
> their inner image in us with their outward image, as though
> with a magical, life-giving finger, and waken that image from
> its profound sleep in order to guide and transform us. These
> historic figures, by fusing with the ancient archetypes, were
> gathered among the eternal symbols of the unconscious, as the
> lights in the darkness of men's souls. This argues for their
> absolute historical validity, for the unconscious cannot really

be fed by inventions and fabrications, for 'all God's works are truth' (Dan. 4:37). The unconscious, always hungry for form, seized upon their coming as a chance of stamping a new and distinct archetype. From them an infinity of forms which were attached to them emanated, flowing into those circling round them. Therefore they alone are alive and immortal, while the millions who have lived on this earth since are completely forgotten. [8]

So pure and holy was the life of the Buddha, Prince Gautama, that Marco Polo was able to write:

If Buddha had been a Christian, he would have been a great saint of our Lord Jesus Christ, so good and pure was the life he led. [9]

[8] H. Zimmer, 'The Significance of Tantric Yoga', in Eranos Yearbook IV, p. 23.
[9] F. Heiler, *History of Religions:* ed. M. Eliade, p. 152.

CHAPTER XVI

THE MYSTERY OF BEING

IN INDIA, WHERE religious thought and devotion are so strong, and where these are marked at their best by mystical aspirations, there are many forms of religious belief. It appears that here, in common with other countries in the East, there is far less exclusiveness than there is in the West, and that it is quite possible for a man to be an adherent of several different persuasions at the same time. It is therefore almost impossible to take a real census of the different religious groups, for the result yields numbers far exceeding the actual population. The traditions are very old, though the Upanishads only date from the 5th century B.C. and are therefore more or less contemporary with many of the Old Testament writings. Because of certain interesting characteristics in Tantric Yoga which seem to run on lines very close to that of the Catholic Church, we will consider briefly some of its less advanced aspects— those which govern the lives of many ordinary Hindus.

The life of the Hindu is bordered with sacraments, and he is surrounded by customs and festive celebrations in the shadow of which he lives. These observances are related to old epic traditions, and their purpose is to guide a man through his life, providing him with symbols and formulas for life in this world. Their psychological function is closely related to that of Yoga. The strange thing about these observances is that they are so apt in what they symbolize. They strike the unconscious in man with the force of symbols, in which they are closely allied to dreams. The observances are

created by the unconscious; they are formed by the collective, suprapersonal spirit of the religious and social community, and their purpose is to appeal to something suprapersonal

within us, to the profounder unconscious. They are intended
to guide it, in order that a man may live in harmony with the
eternal contents that constitute a suprapersonal fate and
exigency transcending the individual, historical situation in
which they mask themselves, the eternal contents that are
common to us and to all living creatures. [1]

This unconscious, to which the observances are addressed, is
full of formed contents: here all the experience and destiny of
man has been deposited in symbols and archetypes. Our deeper
dreams raise up this deposit which lies buried in us and which
is part of the 'collective unconscious' shared by all humanity.
Myths and rites speak to this part of us and bring admonition
and consolation in a way nothing 'rational' could do, because the
rational cannot reach this part of our being. In the unconscious
they encounter something related to them in some mysterious
way— an archetype at work in our depths which, when it is
awakened, is able to respond, and can thus form an *image* that
can gain power over our individuality, which will then adapt
its behaviour to that of the archetype. Such archetypes, when
they are awakened within us, become visible images and effect
our transformation: they rise up in us and become our true
guides. The extraordinary thing is that our conscious will cannot create such guides. The primal archetype alone, with its
timeless validity, evokes within us an image of potential nobility
which moves us to emulation both in our actions and in our
sufferings. In India the power to endure that which is inevitable is regarded as the true wisdom of life, and only the
unconscious is equal to every exigency. This, in Christian
terms, is to share in the sufferings of Christ, to accept in union
with him who would not come down from the Cross, but willed
there to suffer for mankind and for its redemption, all that
comes upon us in the course of our lives, seeing everything as
coming from the hand of God. We are not free to choose these
archetypes for ourselves: they are part of that 'collective
unconscious ' which is part of our heritage. Dr. Zimmer thinks
that we, who are blossoms on the ancient Tree of the West

[1] H. Zimmer, 'The Significance of Tantric Yoga', Eranos Yearbook IV, p. 8.

cannot choose Indian forms for ourselves, for the sap of the Tree
of the West flows in our veins and has passed into our unconscious. Whether the opposite is true, as he maintains, is a very
large question. The 'Buddha' may have passed into the
'unconscious' of the East, but may not that 'unconscious'
find its *perfect* fulfilment, its truest archetype, in the Christ, the
Word made Flesh? We shall turn to this question again later.

In India all the innumerable manifestations of gods and
goddesses are thought of as outward manifestations expressing
the abundance of that inward force known as *shakti*. These
mythical figures are compared to the gestures of man's unconscious. The potentialities they express are latent in all the different individual types, but the germ of these potentialities is not
equally developed. Though we have within us the *seed* of all
things, these seeds do not all germinate and sprout. Our age,
our temperament, and many other factors hold us in the orbit
of the divine or the demonic. All the figures that live in myth
and cult are really corporeal ideas. As variants of archetypes
they lie dormant within us, and serve as models for good or evil.
A whole literature in India has dealt with the paradoxical
relationship between what is pre-eminently *unconscious*— matter
— and *pure consciousness*, the Spirit, which is atemporal, free and
uninvolved in becoming. One of the unexpected results of this
research has been the conclusion that the *unconscious*, moving
apparently by a kind of teleological instinct, imitates the behaviour of the Spirit: that the unconscious behaves in such a way
that its activity seems to *prefigure* the mode of being of the
Spirit. [2] Thus the images of 'flight' and 'ascension' appear
frequently in the world of dreams and imagination, but only
become perfectly intelligible at the level of mysticism and meta-
physics, where they express the ideas of freedom and transcendence.

With regard to the gods of the Brahmans there is no danger
of their refusing to hear and answer prayer after they have
accepted the rites performed in their honour, because they can
be guided by the mechanical practice of the cult. They are

[2] M. Eliade, *Myths, Dreams & Mysteries*, p. 122.

actually subservient to the Brahmans, and man does not feel himself to be at their mercy.   There is no conception here of divine grace, nor was this concept to be found in the original form of Yoga, which probably dates from before the Aryan transmigration.   The Yogi is convinced that he can dominate himself, and does not therefore count on any assistance from the gods.   In fact, he appears to think that, far from helping him, they may envy his power, which he has acquired by his unbending virtue, and that they are much more likely to attempt to destroy this power.

Though the Vedas are looked upon as 'revealed', such spiritual leaders as Jina Mahavira and Buddha Sakyamuni discovered the secret of universal suffering *all by themselves:* it was not revealed to them.   They passed on the secret as to how this suffering might be transformed and overcome, but though their followers shared in their 'secret' there was no question of a revelation.   The Upanishads are closer to revelation because they are surrounded by mystery.   Divine revelation as flowing from grace, however, does not appear till the *Bhagavad-Gita*. Only in Krishnaism, Vaishnaism and Shaivism is there an idea of God inclining to his creatures.   There we do find the thought that only when God approaches to guide and protect the believer is true piety possible.   In these traditions religious life does revolve round the Absolute, in whom, as St. Paul said to the Athenians, 'we live, and move and have our being', instead of centring in the cult rite as it does in Brahmanism and Buddhism. [3]   In the Christian sense pure spirituality is always supernatural: the Spirit bloweth where it listeth.   Man, with his fallen nature, cannot achieve salvation without divine help. In India, on the other hand, there is no idea of original sin or of sanctifying grace by which man's fallen nature may be transcended.   No Hindu could have said 'The Spirit bloweth where it listeth'.

We have seen that the young Hindu is surrounded by various sacramental customs which have as their object the bringing of his young life into relationship with the divine and holy spirits

[3] P. Masson-Oursel, 'The Indian Doctrine of Grace', in Eranos Yearbook II. cp.

rather than with the demonic. This may in a sense be compared with that devotion to the saints which forms part of the religious instruction of most Catholic children, though here this is only part of that comprehensive doctrine of Holy Church in which infants are brought to baptism to be *immersed*, as it were, in the Life of Love of the Blessed Trinity to begin their life 'in Christ Jesus', who is the Way, the Truth, and the Life, by whom alone we have access to the Father. There appears to me to be a vast difference between the Indian and Eastern culture of one's own *interior*, and that faith in Christ which is ours. The Person of Christ, the Incarnate Lord, our pattern and prototype, is the archetype of the christian subconscious. We are baptized into his death, and sealed with his seal, yet his Person does not absorb our personality. He stands over against us, drawing us into union with himself and yet never absorbing us into himself: it is a relationship of love and mutual self-giving. The God of the Christian acts in history and enters into relationship with human beings, and when in Jesus Christ He revealed Himself to us then all history became a manifestation of God and of His ways. All the conceptions of mythical time and mythical space were superseded, and there was a *tremendous revolution*— a revolution too great to have been assimilated in the two thousand years which have passed since then. In Judaism God manifested Himself by choosing His own people and leading them with fatherly care through the centuries in which He prepared the world for the coming of His Son in the flesh. Jesus was part of the history of this world, and he continues to be part of that history in his mystical body the Church. Since the Incarnation took place in history, marking the highest manifestation of the *sacred* in this world, the Christian cannot escape from that concrete, historical life in this world for which Christ died; he cannot simply escape into that time before the *fall* into being, for it is here, in *the world of being*, that he finds on all sides, and in all things, the imprint of the divine love, and learns slowly what it is that lies behind everything in this world. Holy Church surrounds the lives of her children with her life-giving sacraments, and they are thereby brought into growing conformity with their Saviour and prototype, their God, and they look

forward to that blessed time when they shall be like Him, for
they shall see him 'as he is'. That is the true christian 'nostalgia': union with Christ the Beloved, who is the 'new Paradise of
souls' (Prohaska). This way is open to the simplest child: it
is so simple and so true that it is available to all who are not
'offended' in him who is perpetually drawing them into closer
union with himself: 'I, if I be lifted up from the earth will
draw all men unto me' (Jn. 12:32).

Nevertheless, the Eastern outlook should help to throw light
on the meaning of some of Christ's words: 'The kingdom of
heaven is within you.' In the depths of the unconscious we
may meet the 'indwelling Christ'. The techniques employed
in the Christian East— the 'Jesus' prayer and its equivalents—
form a link between East and West, between the Christian
teaching on our life 'in Christ' and the esoteric disciplines of
Buddhism and the other Eastern traditions. We have only to
think of the opening verses of the Fourth Gospel to see how close
the connection must be, since there we are told that Christ is
the 'light that lighteth every man'. Whether we think of a
'fall' which was the result of man's sin and disobedience, or a
'fall' out of the *Timeless* into *time* and *history*, it surely amounts
to much the same thing: it is in each case a 'fall' from the life
of interior union with God, the Everlasting Spirit, and for this
union man has never ceased to hunger and yearn, in whatever
way he may express the thirst which lies at his heart. [4]

'I am come' said Jesus, 'that they might have life, and that
they might have it more abundantly' (Jn. 10:10).

In 1906-7 Dr. C.C. Hall, of Chicago University, delivered
the Barrows lectures in India before a group of Hindu scholars,
whom he addressed with the most profound respect and admiration. He spoke of the sense of the presence of the Unseen
which impressed him so much on returning once more to the
East, which he deeply loved. This was something he felt to be
truly sublime, for it showed that man refused to be wholly

---

[4] Man's spirit 'shows such poverty of nature that it seems to long for the
mere pitiful feeling of the divine in the abstract, and to get refreshment from that,
like a wanderer in the desert craving for the merest mouthful of water. By the
little which can satisfy the needs of the human spirit we can measure the extent of
its loss.' (Hegel, *Phenomenology of Mind*, New York, 1931. Preface.)

immersed in the things of this world and that he reached out unceasingly to the Beyond— towards the inscrutable Mystery of Being. The universal phenomenon of mysticism, which is common to all mankind and which is the raw material of all religion and possibly of all philosophy as well, is that dim consciousness of the *Beyond*, which is part of our nature as human beings. The contemplative life is a glorious heritage of the Indian people, and has given to them what Dr. Hall chose to call the 'Oriental Consciousness'— a consciousness which contains elements the West so direly needs in these days of bustle and stress. It has given them repose, gravity, gentleness, patience, and indifference to material possessions, with a constant remembrance of the Unseen. In the religious thought of the East he found a great preoccupation with the Mystery of Being, and he pointed out that the Creed of Nicea must have been the outcome of influences both Western and Eastern, thus giving us a digest of the religious consciousness of the world: 'God, maker of all things, visible and invisible'.

The Bible he declared to be pre-eminently an Oriental book, breathing a truly Eastern atmosphere. He considered there was a possibility that the courses of those influences which we can trace in the Bible, and which possibly go much further East than we have realized, may actually spring from the same common original as the Vedas, which have determined the religious development of India and the East, since there are many points of contact between the Semitic elements out of which Christianity arose and the Vedic elements out of which the essential features of Indian life evolved. To the great poets of the *Rig-Veda*, as to the prophets of Israel, life in this world was good and glorious and a thing to be desired. They were filled with a warm desire for *life*, and wished for themselves and for their offspring 'a life of a hundred years' (Rig-Veda. 7. 89). Emancipation from finite life was not therefore an element in the earliest Indian thought, which lacked the later pessimistic outlook.

Yet, in spite of his admiration for India and its religious life, Dr. Hall was convinced that Christianity alone was the 'fulfilling religion', and that only by bringing all the rich treasures of its religious consciousness to the feet of Christ would the East find its true fulfilment. He pointed out that the distinction of the Christian religion was that it was a *religion of character*, and not only a *religion of Being*. Here we must stop to consider what this really means. In the first place, to say that it is a religion of character means that Christianity is moral and ethical, in contrast to the mystical religions of the East in which it is frequently asserted that the Ultimate Reality is beyond 'good and evil', and that there is no connection between mystical experience of the divine and the moral law. It is the absolute revelation of a 'Good God' that is the supreme glory of Biblical teaching, and its most perfect development is the Christian faith, for in the New Testament God becomes not less, but more 'holy' than in the Old. In Jesus Christ we see absolute moral perfection, and we believe that here we see the perfect 'image' and 'likeness' of God in man which is that for which man was created. Secondly, Christ has revealed for us for all time the *Nature and Character of God*, the Eternal Ruler and Creator of all things. To 'see Jesus' is to see what our heavenly Father is like in so far as this can be seen and grasped by our limited and created being. Here we see that God's very Nature is love, holiness, compassion. Here, too, we see God's abhorrence of all that is untrue, or evil, or unloving, because all these things are a distortion of the truth. The Bible tells us that we were made to know, and love, and serve God, whose service is perfect freedom, and that we can only find our beatitude in union with Him in love. In Christ we find that peace of God which passes all understanding, the peace that lies behind the changes and chances of this fleeting world. In him we find the joy that lies at the Heart of God— 'Your joy no man taketh from you'. The Christian life is above all a response of love to Love— a relationship between the creature and the Creator, the free surrender of heart and mind to God in Christ.

In bringing to these Hindu scholars the religion of Jesus Christ Dr. Hall said that he did so in the hope that they might help to restore the balance which the Christianity of the West was in danger of losing: an element of that Oriental philosophical culture of the first and second centuries of the Christian era

— a Greek culture with Oriental affinities. The sublime elements in the Oriental consciousness might be the power which would be able to counteract the naturalistic and enfeebled apprehension of Christ which endangers the West, thus giving back to the world 'the fervour, depth and sacredness of Apostolic thought and preaching'[5]. The stupendous power of Christ discerned by those philosophic minds of the earliest centuries of Christianity lifted them to a conception of Divine Life and fellowship fast fading out of the world's consciousness in the glare and noise of Western progress. Hidden in the East he believed there might be such potential apostles of Jesus Christ— men not alien to the philosophy that governed St. John and his immediate successors, who were all accustomed to unworldly contemplation of God. Thus the hungry, fettered souls of men would be restored to their birthright and would be laid under obligation to that which the Eastern approach could restore of the early Christian outlook— that outlook to which Greek thought and culture had contributed so much.

He pointed out that on any count Christ's character and power stood alone in the world— his position is indisputed. It is not the *individuality* of Christ, but rather the absence of it, that makes his greatness so sacred. Here is no forceful individual, but One who reveals to the human race the very character and nature of God, his Father:— 'He that hath seen me hath seen the Father' is the extraordinary claim made by him who was 'meek and lowly of heart'. [6] We cannot affirm the

---

[5] C. C. Hall, *Christ and the Eastern Soul*, p. 165.

[6] Ibid., pp. 168-9. 'The Apostles... recalled the philosophical ideals of a Wisdom and an intelligible Word, coming out of the abyss of the Unknowable to interpret the secrets of the Divine Intelligence, to be a mediator between the Eternal and the ephemeral, the Sum of the thoughts of God, the Idea of Ideas. And as these recollections came to them and set their hearts on fire they perceived that they were divinely kindled, as the burning glass borrows its power from the sun. Through distant Oriental sources they had entered and filled the Greek consciousness, to find, it seemed, their correction and completion in Christ. Therefore they came— through years of reflective experience— to discern His meaning and His nature. For them He was the Loving Spirit of the Lord that filleth all the earth, the Brightness of the Everlasting Light, the Image of His goodness, the Prophet of the Most High, the Mediator, the Heavenly Man, representing before the eyes of God the whole family upon earth. A wondrous interpretation of the facts; an interpretation rich with the mystical spirit of the Oriental Consciousness... After two thousand years of testing in the crucible of experience, the Christian religion comes to us to-day a religion of character founded on the dignity of Christ as the

absolute value of the good in a higher sense than it appears in
Jesus Christ, and therefore we must conclude that

> He is the outspeaking Voice from the shoreless, soundless
> depths of the Infinite Being, confirming goodness as the
> inner essence of the Heart of God. [7]

All that Christ is historically for the life of the world He is
individually for our souls. When the Oriental consciousness
perceives the soul-unifying, redeeming power of Christ, and
gives its own sublime powers to the *religion of character*, as it has
done for thousands of years to the *religions of Being*, then must
come a true recovery of the Spirit of Jesus Christ.

Dr. Hall pleaded with his hearers to receive Jesus Christ as
the 'Logos of the Infinite', as he who enters into the circle of
consciousness to make all things new, purging away sin. He
was convinced that a change was coming in the East when they
would no longer be repelled by the Divinity of Christ, but
would, on the other hand, accept it and help to recover for the
world its true meaning— some of those mysterious depths which
the West is in danger of neglecting. The implications of that
Divinity are so vast, so mysterious, that they are supremely
adapted to the Oriental Consciousness, and that Consciousness
to it. In the Christ, present in the circle of consciousness, the
East might find the answer to all those shadowy questions, those
'subtle approximations of Infinity, those brief and blessed
moments of kinship with God that pass and repass within the
soul that at once preclude expression and suggest certitude'. [8]
Apart from Christ those solemn intimations of the soul's bound-
lessness are bewildering. In him, in Christ, the soul gains

Moral Revelation of God, the answer to the highest aspirations of man's soul.
Like gold, thrice refined, both elements, the historical and the mystical, have
been subject to every test that the wisdom, pride, or sin of man can apply, and
both remain to-day. By hatred and love, by good report and evil report, by
prosperity and adversity, by learning and culture, by ignorance and superstition,
by science, by philosophy and ethics have these elements been tested until the
essential truths of the historical and mystical in the Christian religion have been
completely proven, and have taken their place among the things that cannot
be shaken.'
   [7] Ibid., p. 199.
   [8] Ibid., p. 199.

insight into its own ideal and receives the answers to its own questions and aspirations, and then, reflecting as in a mirror the glory of the Lord, it is changed into his own image. This Christ, whom we discover in the circle of consciousness, and who is so absolutely one with us that we are members of his Body, is no other than the Word of the Infinite, of God mediating to us the truth of our oneness with Him in Christ. It is the revelation of the Heart of God, affirming Love to be the very essence of the Divine, where pain and sacrifice appear in a new light. Dr. Hall was versed in the Indian holy writings and was able to trace in them passages that might well be prophetic. In the *Rig-Veda* he found a whole hymn addressed and devoted to the Word, the Logos, and in *Maha Bharata* he also saw real *Logos* teaching:

The Eternal Word, without beginning, without end, was uttered by the Self-existent (8.533).

He claimed that through the Crucified Humanity of Christ we rise into the region of the Infinite, and touch the very Heart of God:

the Fountain of holy love, out of which all holy love in us has emerged as the secondary and responsive image of Himself. [9]

[9] Ibid., p. 203.

CHAPTER XVII

THE MYSTERY OF THE CROSS

CHRISTIANITY STEMS FROM the Death of Christ upon the Cross on the first Good Friday. The Passion-narratives are the very core of the Gospels— in a sense their starting-point. All else in them probably grew up around this one fact of the Suffering and Death and Resurrection of the Lord. St. Paul, too, begins his declaration of the gospel with the death of Christ (1 Cor. 15:3). He who had been so cruelly put to death, was risen, and alive for evermore. He, Jesus, whose word and works and miracles had made so deep an impression on those who lived closest to him that it had wrung from St. Peter the confession 'Thou art the Christ, the Son of the Living God', had now also fulfilled that other mysterious prophecy of the Suffering Servant of Isaiah 53. While he had gone about doing good during the short years of his active ministry it had seemed to them that many a prophecy was being fulfilled: the blind received their sight, the deaf heard, the lame rose up and walked, devils were cast out, and the dead raised to life. Now there was something further. In his Epistle St. Peter was able to use the picture of the Suffering Servant and to show that it had been perfectly fulfilled in a *Person*— the 'great Shepherd and Bishop of our souls'— who by his love and his meekness had on the Cross won the victory over every form of evil, making a 'show of them openly, triumphing over them in it' (Col. 2:15). Somewhere Professor Oscar Cullman has suggested that it would really be more correct for the Church's year to begin with Good Friday and Easter, rather than with the much later Advent and Christmas: later, that is, in the calendar of the Church, since it is on the Death and Resurrection of Christ that our faith is primarily based. In the earliest Church there was but one great Feast: that of the *Pascha*, which celebrated together the saving Death and the glorious rising from the dead.

Though this Death on the Cross is a fact of history— a stark and terrible punishment meted out under Roman criminal law— it is also a mystery which encompasses all the history of the world.   Here the Christian sees the focal point of all history and of all life— the 'Centre' where God and man meet, where this world and the great Unseen world cross and interpenetrate.   All history that went before was a preparation for this, all history that follows flows from this point and is in some measure influenced by it.   Here was something wholly above and beyond worldly wisdom and understanding, some-thing enacted in the divine sphere— a Mystery.   In this Mystery a *divine reality* broke through into the world.   It was all so simple as to be 'foolishness to the Greeks' and to the Jews a stumbling-block, but then is it not, as Professor Kerenyi once said, the

secret of every true and great mystery that it is simple? [1]

The simplest things have always provided symbols for that which is beyond all human understanding, that which reaches down to the depths of life and being, and points up into the heights, into the divine.   We have thought of the symbolism of the Tree of Life and of the waters flowing from Paradise to water all the cosmos, of light and darkness, of sun and moon, of sacred marriage, of the heavenly ladder, of a 'centre', whether it be a stone or a tree, a house or a temple, of the ear of wheat, all so simple and so much part of the world in which we have been placed, and yet providing adequate expression for that deep 'secret' which lies behind this world of sense, and into which man is perpetually drawn in one way or another, sensing a mysterious 'beyond', which lends to this world a wonder, a something that fills man with nostalgic longings. We speak of the 'Holy Grail' of Arthurian romance, and the veil of this world wears thin; we think of St. Francis and his Lady Poverty, and our hearts are stirred as by something not of

[1] C. Kerenyi, *Essay on the Science of Mythology* (London 1956, p. 256).

this world.   Because they have this quality of mystery these legends never die, since they speak to something deep in the heart of man.

In the Cross there are again those simple and ordinary things: a rough wooden Cross, the nails piercing hands and feet, a spear opening a wound in the heart of the dead Christ from which flow streams of living blood and water, to bring salvation to every quarter of the globe.   Into that open Heart we enter, and there find our Refuge and our Home, for it is the Heart of our Maker and our God, who is always and at all times drawing us into union with Himself.   Here, in all the simple and tragic details we see the supreme glory of God manifested for all time, for here we see in very truth that

> God so loved the world, that He gave his only-begotten Son, that whosoever believeth in him should not perish, but have everlasting life.   For God sent not his Son into the world to condemn the world; but that the world through Him might be saved (John 3:16-17).

As Moses lifted up the brazen serpent in the wilderness and all who looked upon that serpent were healed, so the Son of Man was lifted up that all who believed on him 'should not perish, but have everlasting life'.

The sign of the Cross, the mystery of the Cross, which so fascinated the early Christians, is always the mystery of the *Person* of Christ Crucified, for every really perfect symbol is something that lives and dies, 'something transient' (Buber). We glory in the Cross only because it was upon a Cross that our beloved Lord redeemed us, and showed us for all time that, having loved his own in this world, he 'loved them unto the end' (John 13: 1).   He who died and rose again is 'the same yesterday, to-day and for ever' (Heb. 13:8).   He is Love utterly triumphant over every form of evil, Love utterly compassionate, who *willed* to lay down his life for us in order to bring us thereby to union with God, our heavenly Father. Yet we must always remember that though Jesus told us that he was the Way, he is also the *End*.   St. Augustine insisted that, in going *by* Jesus as the Way we were also going *to* him, and not to another by him.

The early Christians saw in the Cross a mystery the sense of which has been largely lost to us, even if it is also true that in some ways we have penetrated more deeply into certain aspects of it, since we have behind us nearly two thousand years of *experience* of the Cross of Christ: years in which countless souls, great and simple, high and lowly, have lived their lives under the shadow of the Cross and in its strength, and have found there grace to guide them through all the trials and perplexities of life.   On the Cross the beginning and the end of the world come together, for he who died thereon is both the very 'Word of God' by whom all things were made, and that 'Omega' point to which all creation moves as to its appointed end. In the vision of St. John the Seer this thought is given scriptural expression.   He saw 'the Lamb as it had been slain' in the midst of the throne of heaven (Rev. 5:6), and heard the heavenly hosts sing:

> Thou wast slain, and hast redeemed us to God by thy blood out of every kindred, and tongue, and people and nation, and hast made us unto our God kings and priests; and we shall reign on the earth.   And I beheld and I heard the voice of many angels round about the throne and the beasts and the elders: and the number of them was ten thousand times ten thousand, and thousands of thousands; saying with a loud voice, Worthy is the Lamb that was slain to receive power, and riches, and wisdom and strength, and honour, and glory and blessing.   And every creature which is in heaven, and on the earth, and under the earth, and such as are in the sea, and all that are in them, heard I saying, Blessing and honour, and glory, and power, be unto him that sitteth upon the throne, and unto the Lamb for ever and ever (Rev. 5:9-13).

Plato, in his *Timaeus*, had spoken of the world soul revealed in the X in the heavens.   The early Christians applied this thought to the crucified Word of God, seeing here a prophetic intimation of his Cross, and concluding that the whole cosmos was built to revolve round the Cross of Christ.   St. Justin applied this passage in Plato to Christ, and though he only mentions it in passing it was obviously a familiar conception. St. Irenaeus brought this idea into a passage which is one of the most famous of all early Christian texts on the Cross as gathering up into itself all the history both of the Bible and of creation. [2] Those early Christians saw in the four ends of the Cross the four dimensions of the cosmos, and with St. Paul sought to enter into something of the mystery of that which is beyond human comprehension:

> That ye, being rooted and grounded in love, may be able to comprehend with all saints what is the breadth, and length, and depth and height; and to know the love of Christ, which passeth knowledge, that ye might be filled with all the fulness of God (Eph. 3:17-19).

The Cross is the simple sign of something vast and unknowable; it gathers up and sums up all things in itself. To quote from St. Irenaeus, whose writings so greatly influenced the formulation of later Christian doctrine:

> The Creator of the world is truly the Word of God; and this is our Lord, who in the last time was made man, existing in this world, and who in an invisible manner contains all things created, and is inherent in the entire creation, since the Word of God governs and arranges all things; and therefore He came to His own in a visible manner, and was made flesh, and hung upon the tree, that He might sum up all things in Himself. [3]

---

[2] 'So then by the obedience by which he obeyed even unto death, hanging on the tree, He put away the old disobedience which was wrought in the tree. Now seeing He is the Word of God Almighty, who in unseen wise in our midst is universally extended in all the world, and encompasses its length and breadth and height and depth— for by the Word of God the whole universe is ordered and disposed— in it is crucified the Son of God, inscribed crosswise upon it all: for it is right that He, being made visible, should set upon all things visible the sharing of His Cross, that He might show His operation on visible things through a visible form. For He it is who illumines the height that is in the heavens; and encompasses the deep that is beneath the earth; and stretches and spreads out the length from east to west; and steers across the breadth of north and south; summoning all that are scattered in every quarter to the knowledge of the Father.' (Irenaeus: *Epideixis*, I, 34. trans. from the Armenian by J. Armitage Robinson, *The Demonstration of the Apostolic Preaching*, London, 1920, pp. 101, 2).

[3] *Adv. Haer. V*, 18, 3. Ante Nicene Library, Edinburgh, 1869, pp. 105, 6.

This thought was like a thread running through the early Christian writings. We find it in the catechetical lectures addressed by St. Cyril of Jerusalem to his candidates for baptism, given on the historic site of the Crucifixion itself. [4] This vision of the Cross as a 'cosmic' victory was especially perpetuated among the Byzantines. 'O Cross' wrote Andrew of Crete, 'thou atonement of the cosmos, thou limit of the world, thou height of heaven, thou depth of earth, thou bond of creation, thou width of all that is visible, thou breath of the Oikoumene'. [5] St. Augustine, too, often spoke of the cosmic dimensions of the Cross. 'The sign of the Cross holds together the heavenly mechanism' wrote Firmicus Maternus, 'strengthens the foundation of the earth, leads those who hold it in their hearts to life'.

It was typical of the thought of the Early Church to see in the Cross the means by which the whole universe might be brought to heaven, to see the 'sign' of the Cross imprinted on all creation. They saw this sign everywhere, even in inanimate nature and in the implements of daily life: they saw it in the shape of the human body, in agricultural implements made in the form of a cross and in the masts of ships. In the second century St. Justin wrote:

> The sea cannot be traversed unless the sign of victory, which is called a sail, remain fast in the ship; the land is not ploughed without it; similarly diggers and mechanics do not do their work except with tools of this form. The human figure differs from the irrational animals precisely in this, that a man stands erect and can stretch out his hands. [6]

Three centuries later Maximus of Turin said in a sermon:

> Magnificent is the mystery of the Cross! For in this sign the whole earth is saved. A symbol of this mystery is the sail that hangs on the mast of a ship as though it were Christ raised on the Cross... Even the vault of heaven is shaped in the form of

---

[4] Cat 13, 28 (P.G. XXXIII, 805 B)
[5] *In Exultationem sanctae Crucis* (P.G. XCVII, 1021 C).
   Apologia, I, 55.

a cross. And man, when he walks along, when he raises his arms: he describes a cross, and for this reason we should pray with outstretched arms, in order that we ourselves with the posture of our limbs may imitate the suffering of our Lord. [7]

Nor was the Cross only the epitome of all creation, it was also the true fulfilment of all the Old Testament writings: this is the Tree of life in the Garden of Paradise, this is that 'wood' whereby Noah was saved from the waters of the Flood. Here is the 'promised land', for though Joshua brought his people over Jordan into the land of Canaan, that was not the true *end* of the promise, that was not the true *rest* held out to the Children of Israel, whereby they should enter into the eternal *Sabbath* of God, for, says the writer to the Hebrews, 'If Joshua had given them rest, then would he not afterwards have spoken of another day.' This is the true 'ladder' which Jacob saw, this is the 'tree of life to them that lay hold of her', which is one of the forms under which wisdom is spoken of in the Proverbs (3:18).

In the Old Testament, because man was not yet ready to see and comprehend the true light that shone upon the world in Christ, everything was cloaked in images and symbols. St. Augustine saw in the rending of the veil of the Temple at the Death of Christ a sign that what had hitherto been hidden might now be revealed. We will consider for the moment but one of these 'symbols' of the Old Testament, since it bears especially on our theme: the wood of the Tree of Life in Paradise. The Jews saw in this Tree in the garden, watered by the four rivers of Paradise, a symbol of the Messiah, for this Tree symbolizes the true Wisdom.

St. John the Divine, in the great Christian Apocalypse, says, 'To him that overcometh will I give to eat of the tree of life, which is in the midst of the Paradise of God' (Rev. 2:7). The last chapters of the Bible speak of Paradise: the Scriptures, indeed, begin and end with this thought. St. John saw 'a new heaven and a new earth: for the first heaven and the first earth were passed away; and there was no more sea'. The sea, with all its varied symbolic meanings, always held an

---

[7] *Homilia 50: De cruce Domini* (PL, LVII, 341 ff).

element of the uncertain and unpredictable, something to be feared, and therefore when St. John says 'there shall be no more sea', he means that all fear and all uncertainty which bring so much suffering to the lives of men will be done away.

> And I, John, saw the holy city, new Jerusalem, coming down from God out of heaven, prepared as a bride adorned for her husband... and I saw no temple therein: for the Lord God Almighty and the Lamb are the temple of it.   And the city had no need of the sun, neither of the moon, to shine in it: for the glory of God did lighten it, and the Lamb is the light thereof (Rev. 21:22f).

There is no night in this city, and the gates are never shut by day, and nothing defiled shall enter into this pure and holy place, but only those who have 'washed their robes in the blood of the Lamb'.   Then comes the final picture of the paradisal garden:

> And he showed me a pure river of water of life, clear as crystal, proceeding out of the throne of God and of the Lamb.   In the midst of the street of it, and on either side of the river, was there the tree of life, which bare twelve manner of fruits, and yielded her fruit every month: and the leaves of the tree were for the healing of the nations.   And there shall be no more curse: but the throne of God and of the Lamb shall be in it; and his servants shall serve him: and they shall see his face; and his name shall be in their foreheads.   And there shall be no night there; and they shall need no candle, neither light of the sun; for the Lord God giveth them light, and they shall reign for ever and ever (Rev. 22: 1-5).

This is the *Paradise* to which the Christian looks forward with confident hope, for as Jesus hung upon the Cross on Calvary a malefactor, crucified by his side, turned to him with a last, sudden act of faith and a prayer for mercy:

> Lord, remember me when thou comest to thy kingdom.
> And Jesus said unto him, Verily I say unto thee, Today shalt thou be with me in Paradise (St. Luke 23:43).

On the Cross, in the midst of mortal pain, the Lord spoke of that Paradise to which the hearts of men have so often turned, and for which through the ages they have yearned. 'With me in Paradise': that is the end of all Christian hope and of all Christian desire, to be 'with Christ'. And this is not something to be attained only in 'ecstasy' or after death, but something that may begin here and now, in this, life for, says St. Paul, 'Your life is hid with Christ in God' (Col. 3:3).

At baptism every Christian child is brought into union with Christ in His Death (Rom. 6:3) and by the grace of the Holy Spirit he is conformed more and more to the likeness of his Saviour, in the measure in which he corresponds with the grace outheld. It is a life of growing intimacy of person with *Person*, which begins here in this life, but which is destined to come to its full fruition only in the life beyond the veil. This is the hope held out to every true follower of Christ, whose life is nourished by the Bread of life during the time of this earthly pilgrimage. To be 'with Christ' is the end of all desire for Christ's lovers. Julian of Norwich summed it up perfectly when she said simply, 'I took Jesus to my heaven'.

The Pseudo-Chrysostom, in an Easter sermon, gathered up all these thoughts on the Mystery of the Cross in glowing words:

> This tree as broad as the heavens has grown up from the earth to heaven. Immortal tree, it extends from heaven to earth. It is the fixed pivot of the universe, the fulcrum of all things, the foundation of the world, the cardinal point of the cosmos. It binds together all the multiplicity of human nature. It is held together by invisible nails of the spirit in order to retain its bond with the godhead. It touches the highest summits of heaven and with its feet holds fast the earth, and it encompasses the vast middle atmosphere in between with its immeasurable arms. [8]

Not only is the Cross the Tree of Life, it is also the bringer of light. The Paschal Candle is a symbol of the Crucified

---

[8] *De Pascha, Homilia 6* (P.G. LIX, 743-46).

Christ, and the five grains of incense which are inserted into it symbolize the five wounds. Since the Cross is also the Tree of Life the candle is adorned with flowers. As the Candle is borne up the aisle after the blessing of the New Fire on Easter night it is thrice held aloft with the triumphant cry 'Light of Christ', whereupon the people kneel and sing 'Thanks be to God'. The Candle is dipped into the baptismal font, suggesting that by the power of Christ Crucified the water will give eternal life to all who are baptized therein. Then the water of the font is scattered to the four quarters of the church, symbolizing the four quarters of the world through which the new 'waters of Paradise' will flow that new life and hope may spring up as flowers wherever they go, transforming earth into heaven.

Here is utmost simplicity and impenetrable mystery, for the life of union with Jesus Christ and Him Crucified, knowing that we are 'in him', in 'Christ', is something far more wonderful than any pure God-mysticism can ever be: it is wholly supernatural, bringing us into that life of love of the Blessed Trinity into which we are brought by Jesus, who made the perfect sacrifice, the true surrender of *self* to the Father, which makes it possible for us to come to our Heavenly Father by and through and in Him. Because we have inherited a *fallen* nature— a nature distorted and perverted by sin— it is this very simplicity that it is so extremely difficult for us to grasp and lay hold of. Yet this simplicity is the *secret* of the Biblical writings from those first words God spoke to Adam, 'Where art thou?', to those blessed words of the Incarnate Lord:

Come unto me all ye that labour and are heavy laden and I will give you rest (St. Matt. 11: 28).
Learn of me, for I am meek and lowly of heart, and ye shall find rest unto your souls. For my yoke is easy and my burden is light (ibid. 29-30).
Behold, I stand at the door and knock: if any man will hear my voice, and open the door, I will come in to him, and will sup with him, and he with me (Rev. 3:20).

St. John, looking upon the white-robed throng around the throne of God asked who they might be:

> These are they which have come out of great tribulation and have washed their robes in the blood of the Lamb. Therefore are they before the throne of God, and serve him day and night in his temple: and he that sitteth on the throne shall dwell among them. They shall hunger no more, neither thirst any more... For the Lamb which is in the midst of the throne shall feed them, and shall lead them unto living fountains of waters: and God shall wipe away all tears from their eyes (Rev. 7:15ff).

It is therefore surely fitting that on this note the Bible ends:

> Even so, come, Lord Jesus (Rev. 22:22).

May we not conclude that all the longing for Paradise which has marked and still does mark the human race as being 'in' the world yet not wholly 'of' it, springs from the hidden, magnetic attraction of the Love of Christ, by whom all things were made and by whom they consist, and for union with whom we were destined from the very foundation of the world?

INDEX